The Atrocities
of the Pirates

CONTENTS

THE ATROCITIES

OF THE

PIRATES;

BEING

A FAITHFUL NARRATIVE

OF THE

UNPARALLELED SUFFERINGS

ENDURED BY THE AUTHOR DURING HIS CAPTIVITY
AMONG THE PIRATES OF

THE ISLAND OF CUBA;

WITH AN ACCOUNT OF THE

EXCESSES AND BARBARITIES

OF THOSE

INHUMAN FREEBOOTERS,

BY AARON SMITH,

TOGETHER WITH A COPIOUS AND EXPLICIT REPORT OF HIS
SUBSEQUENT TRIAL AT THE OLD BAILEY.

DECORATED THROUGHOUT WITH
ENGRAVINGS BY ERIC RAVILIOUS

THE GOLDEN COCKEREL PRESS
MCMXXIX

INTRODUCTION

Aaron Smith was my great, great grandfather. He was an honest merchant seaman forced against his will to join a pirate crew. We know for certain that he was taken on 7th July 1822 and Royal Naval records tell us he had escaped from the pirate vessel by the end of September at the latest. Yet those few months shattered the future he had planned for himself and his fiancée and left him maimed for life. He was brought back to England in irons for trial at the Old Bailey with the Attorney General leading for the prosecution. Had he been found guilty, he would have ended his life at Execution Dock at Wapping.

He wrote an account of his experiences and this was published in 1824. The book was re-printed in 1929 by the famous Golden Cockerel Press and it gives the most gruesome description of pirate cruelty. It shows piracy as the frightening, bestial activity that it has always been. There was never anything of Errol Flynn's Hollywood about it. Men like Aaron Smith – masters of trades the pirates needed (he was a navigator and accepted as a ship's surgeon) – and the carpenter whose appalling fate is recounted by Aaron, were kidnapped from legitimate ships, forced to serve the pirates and then killed when they had served their purpose.

I found out that I was Aaron Smith's descendant only by accident and only recently. I will tell that story and take Aaron's account beyond what he knew or could foresee - how he became a wanted man and was sought by the Royal Navy as a notorious criminal, what happened to the pirate schooner and how he was again put on trial for his life in 1829.

But first you should read Aaron's own account - *The Atrocities of the Pirates*.

Robert S. Redmond
Member of Parliament for Bolton West,
June 1970 to October 1974

ORIGINAL PREFACE

The following narrative is so ample and circumstantial in its details, and the unparalleled barbarities witnessed and endured by Mr. Smith during his captivity by the Pirates of Cuba are so clearly narrated, that it may appear scarcely necessary to detain the Reader by pre-fixing anything by way of Preface. But the Author of the subsequent pages, who is now again employed in the duties of his profession, having, before he quitted England, committed his 'plain unvarnished tale' to the care of a friend, that friend conceives he cannot perform a more acceptable service to a brave and mer-itorious, though unfortunate, man, than by submitting the same to the notice of a humane and generous public; while, it is humbly conceived, no portion of that public will read the narrative without feeling emotions of a two-fold and opposite kind – pity for a man who underwent such unmerited sufferings, and indignation at the base conduct of those who, with the means in their power, neglected to vindicate his injured honor, & to wipe off the stigma of his being a willing accessory to the unparalleled atrocities herein detailed.

Aaron Smith was, on the 19th of December 1823, tried, on a charge of Piracy, before the High Court of Admiralty; and such was the zeal of his prosecutors to make an example of a British seaman who had become, however involuntarily, the associate of a gang of Pirates, that, notwithstanding all the perils & hardships he had undergone, he narrowly escaped an ignominious death – and that, too, by the laws of his own country, in whose service his previous life had been passed with credit and honor![1]

The crime for which Aaron Smith was tried, is undoubtedly one of the deepest turpitude, and one at which his honest mind revolted; but those who peruse the following pages, will see that he was so completely in the power of that demoniacal crew of Pirates, so involved in the meshes of their inextricable net, that neither bravery nor artifice, neither skill nor enter-prise, could effect his deliverance. While groaning under the weight of his own sufferings, and looking forwards only to the means of escape, he was com-pelled to assume an air of satisfaction, and to join in the desperate acts of those freebooters. To elude their vigilance, and to avoid the terrible effects of their vengeance, it was imperative on him to act precisely in the way he did act; any other line of conduct would, in fact, have subjected him to a horrible death, pre-ceded perhaps by tortures at which the stoutest heart would have trembled.

[1] *The brief outline of the trial given in the preface to the original edition is here omitted, as the full account, taken from the Morning Chronicle of December 20th, 1823, is now printed at the end of this volume.*

THE ATROCITIES
OF THE PIRATES

In the month of June 1821, I embarked on board the merchant ship *Harrington*, and proceeded on a voyage to the West Indies. Subsequent events, however, induced me to resign my situation in that vessel and devote myself to other pursuits. After having passed nearly two years in that part of the world, and finding my health somewhat impaired by the climate, I became anxious to see my family once more, and made the necessary arrangements for my return to England. Being then at Kingston, in the island of Jamaica, I communicated my wishes to a Captain Talbot, an intimate friend, who very kindly undertook to forward my views, and introduced and recommended me to Mr. Lumsden, the master of the merchant brig *Zephyr*, which vessel was at that time waiting for freight to London. In consequence of this introductory recommendation, I entered into an agreement with that person to accompany him as his first mate; and about the middle of April, 1822, I commenced the duties of my office. The season that year had been very unfavourable to the planters; the crops had in many instances failed, and freights were in consequence very scarce. The lading of the *Zephyr* therefore proceeded very slowly, and I became daily more anxious for my return.

In the mean time I embarked in a trifling speculation, and purchased and shipped a quantity of coffee on board the brig on my own account; from time to time consulting and advising with Mr. Lumsden as to the best methods of completing our lading. Some time, however, still elapsed before we could attain our object; and during this interval I discovered so many unamiable traits in the character of that person as to cause very unfavourable impressions on my mind towards him. His ignorance & want of education betrayed themselves on almost every occasion; nor was I surprised at the discovery when I was afterwards informed that he had been originally bred to the coal trade, and had been nearly all his life employed in that capacity.

Towards the latter end of June, we had completed our cargo; &, having taken on board our passengers, who consisted of a Captain Cowper, five or six children, and a black woman as a servant, we sailed on the 29th, and proceeded down to Port Royal, where we anchored for the night. Mr. Lumsden, with some friends belonging to the children, & a lady of colour, at whose house he had lodged during his stay on the island, followed the vessel in a boat, and came on board at Port Royal. The boat was then sent for another passenger; and, on his arrival, the person who had accompanied Mr. Lumsden returned on shore.

On the following morning we weighed anchor and left the port, and, having discharged the pilot, proceeded on our voyage, with a moderate breeze and fine weather; but very soon afterwards encountered strong north-easterly winds, accompanied by a heavy swell from the eastward. Mr. Lumsden now seemed anxious to consult me as to future proceedings, and asked me whether I should deem it advisable for him to ply for the windward, or to bear up for the leeward passage. The opinion which I had formed of his character rendered me unwilling to hazard my advice, as I did not wish to have any responsibility thrown on me hereafter, from what might be the result of his own ignorance and want of skill. As, however, I could not, consistently with my duty, altogether refuse my opinion, I confined my answer merely to pointing out the advantages and disadvantages of each, without evincing any prepossession in favor of either. The windward passage, I informed him, might prolong the voyage, but the leeward would expose us to the risk of being plundered by pirates, and, perhaps, the total destruction of the vessel, of which the accounts in the daily journals gave too melancholy warnings; & therefore I should recommend him to be guided by his own judgment and experience. Without considering much upon the subject, he decided upon the latter, notwithstanding the perils to which such a measure might expose him.

In consequence of this determination, we steered for the Great Caamans, which islands the heavy sailing of the *Zephyr* & the unusual lightness of the winds prevented us from reaching until the fourth day. The inhabitants came off to us in canoes, & we purchased a few parrots, some turtles, and a quantity of shells. From thence we steered for Cape Saint Antonio, the south-west point of the island of Cuba; and on our passage spoke to a schooner belonging to St. John's, New Brunswick, on her return from Kingston. This vessel had made an unsuccessful attempt to ply for the windward passage, and had abandoned it on the fifth or sixth day. We parted company in the night, and on the following morning made Cape Saint Antonio: the wind was still light and the weather fine. Having got round the Cape, we stood to eastward, and the breezes freshened and became more favorable. At daylight on the following morning, we discovered two sail a-head, standing the same course, and, in the forenoon, the day being remarkably clear and fine, took a very good observation of the sun's altitude.

At two o'clock, P.M., while walking the deck in conversation with Captain Cowper, I discovered a schooner standing out towards us from the land; she bore a very suspicious appearance, and I immediately went up aloft with my telescope to examine her more closely. I was instantly convinced that she was a pirate, and mentioned it to Cowper, who coincided with me, and we deemed it proper to call Mr. Lumsden from below & inform him. When he came on deck we pointed out the schooner and stated our suspicions, recommending him to alter his course and avoid her. We were at this moment about six leagues from Cape Roman, which bore S.E. by E. Never did ignorance, with its concomitant obstinacy, betray itself more strongly than on this occasion; he rejected our advice and refused to alter his course, and was infatuated enough to suppose, that, because he bore the English flag, no one would dare to molest him. To this obstinacy and infatuation I must attribute all my subsequent misfortunes — the unparalleled cruelties which I have suffered — the persecutions and prosecutions which I have undergone — the mean and wanton insults which have been heaped upon me — and the villany and dishonesty to which I have been exposed from the author of them all; who, not satisfied with having occasioned my sufferings, would have basely taken advantage of them to defraud my friends of what little of my property had escaped the general plunder.

In about half an hour after this conversation, we began to discover that the deck of the schooner was full of men, and that she was beginning to hoist out her boats. This circumstance greatly alarmed Mr. Lumsden, and he ordered the course to be altered two points, but it was then too late, for the stranger was within gun-shot. In a short time she was within hail, and, in English, ordered us to lower our stern boat and send the captain on board of her. Mr. Lumsden either did not understand the order, or pretended not to do so, and the corsair, for such she now proved to be, fired a volley of musketry. This increased his terror, which he expressed in hurried exclamations of Aye, aye! Oh, Lord God! and then gave orders to lay the main yard aback. A boat from the pirate now boarded the *Zephyr*, containing nine or ten men, of a most ferocious aspect, armed with muskets, knives, and cutlasses who immediately took charge of the brig, and ordered Captain Cowper, Mr. Lumsden, the ship's carpenter, and myself, to go on board the pirate, hastening our departure by repeated blows with the flat part of their cutlasses over our backs, and threatening to shoot us. The rapidity of our movements did not give us much time for consideration; and, while we were rowing towards the corsair, Mr. Lumsden remarked that he had been very careless in leaving the books, which contained the account of all the money on board, on the cabin table. The captain of the pirate ordered us on deck immediately on our arrival. He was a man of most uncouth and savage appearance, about five feet six inches in height, stout in proportion, with aquiline nose, high cheek bones, a large mouth, and very large full eyes. His complexion was sallow, and his hair black, and he appeared to be about two and thirty years of age. In his appearance he very much resembled an Indian, and I was afterwards informed that his father was a Spaniard and his mother a Yucatan Squaw. He first addressed Mr. Lumsden, & inquired in broken English what the vessels were that he saw a-head. On being informed that they were French merchantmen, he gave orders for all hands to go in chase. The *Zephyr* was observed in the mean time to make sail and stand in the direction of Cape Roman.

The captain now addressed himself to Mr. Lumsden on the subject of his cargo, which he was informed consisted of sugars, rum, coffee, arrow root, dye woods, & co. He then severally inquired who and what we were; and then whether we had spoken any vessel on our passage. On being informed of the schooner from New Brunswick, he asked if we thought she had specie on board. We told him that those vessels in general sold their cargoes for cash, and he seemed very anxious to learn whether she was a-head or a-stern of us, and whether she was armed. Mr. Lumsden now entreated the captain to make a signal to the *Zephyr* not to stand nearer to the land, as he was apprehensive of her going on shore, and was told that he need not be under any alarm, as there was a very experienced pilot on board of her. He was, however, dissatisfied with this reply, and repeated his entreaty, when the other, in a menacing tone, enjoined silence, and went forward. In a short time he returned and questioned Mr. Lumsden as to what money he had on board, and when told that there was none, he replied, 'Do not imagine that I am fool, Sir; I know that all vessels going to Europe have specie on board; & if you will give up what you have, you shall proceed on your voyage without further molestation.' Mr. Lumsden repeated his answer, and the pirate declared that if the money was not produced, he would detain the *Zephyr*, throw her cargo overboard, and, if any was found concealed, he would burn her with every soul belonging to her. He then asked whether there were any candles, wine, or porter, on board; and Mr. Lumsden foolishly replied, not any that he could spare, without appearing to consider that we were in his power, and that he could if he pleased possess himself of any thing he might wish without consulting his convenience.

The night was at this time fast approaching, and the breeze had begun to die away. The captain appeared to despair of coming up with his chase, which we could now clearly perceive to be a ship, and a brig, and asked Captain Cowper and myself whether he should be able to overtake them before dark. We replied in the negative, and he then gave orders to shorten sail and stand towards the *Zephyr*. The pirates then began to prepare for supper, and were very liberal in serving out spirits to our boat's crew, and also offered us a share, or wine if we preferred it, but we declined both.

The captain now turned to me and said, that, as he was in a bad state of health and none of his ship's company understood navigation, he should detain me for the purpose of navigating the schooner. I tried as much as possible to conceal my emotions at this intimation, and endeavoured to work upon his feelings by telling him that I was married and had three children — that they, together with my wife and aged parents, were anxiously expecting me at home; and represented, in as pathetic language as I could, the misery & distraction which it would cause them, beseeching him to spare my wife and children, and not bring down the grey hairs of my unfortunate parents with sorrow to the grave. But I appealed to a monster, devoid of all feeling, inured to crime, and hardened in iniquity. Mr. Lumsden in the mean time interfered, and hoped that he would not deprive him of my services: but he savagely told him, 'If I do not keep him, I shall keep you.' This threat evidently alarmed and agitated him, and he seemed to regret the part he had taken.

A few minutes, however, displayed the unfeeling & selfish character of this man in the strongest light. 'Mr. Smith,' said he, turning to me, 'for God's sake do not importune the captain, or he will certainly take me: you are a single man, but I have a large family dependent upon me, who will become orphans and be utterly destitute. The moment I am liberated, I shall proceed to the Havannah, and despatch a man of war in search of the corsair, and at the same time publish to the world the manner in which you have been forcibly detained. Nay, I will represent the whole affair at Lloyd's; and, should the pirate be captured hereafter, and you found on board, no harm shall befall you. Whatever property you have shall be safely delivered to your family, and mine will for ever bless you for the kind and generous act.' During this address he was much affected, and the tears streamed from his eyes. I sympathized in his feelings, and replied, that I hoped that neither of us would be detained; but if the lot must fall upon one, under these circumstances, and on these conditions, I would consent to become the victim. This declaration calmed his agitated spirits; but little did I think of the treachery and duplicity that had been masked beneath them, and which subsequent events have too clearly demonstrated.

Supper having been prepared, the captain and his officers, six or seven in number, sat down to it, and invited us to join them, which, for fear of giving offence and exciting their brutality, we did. Our supper consisted of garlic and onions chopped fine and mixed up with bread in a bowl, for which there was a general scramble, every one helping himself as he pleased, either with his fingers or any instrument with which he happened to be supplied.

During supper Mr. Lumsden begged to be allowed to go on board the *Zephyr* to the children, as he was fearful that they would be alarmed at our absence and the presence of strangers, in which request I joined; but he replied, that no one would injure them, and that, as soon as the two vessels came to an anchor, he would accompany us on board.

The corsair was at this time fast approaching the *Zephyr*, when the Captain ordered a musket to be fired, and then tacked in shore; the signal was immediately answered, & the brig followed our movements. One of our boat's crew was then ordered to the lead, with directions to give notice the moment he found soundings, and the captain then inquired if we had any Americans on board as seamen. He expressed himself very warmly against them, and declared he would kill all belonging to that nation in revenge for the injuries that he had sustained at their hands, one of his vessels having been lately taken and destroyed by them; adding, at the same time, that if he discovered that we had concealed the fact from him, he would punish us equally. To the Americans he said that he should never give quarter; but as all nations were hostile to Spain, he would attack all.

The man at the lead, during this conversation, gave notice of soundings in fourteen fathoms, and the captain ordered the boat down, and told Mr. Lumsden he would accompany him on board his vessel. The men we had brought were ordered into the boat, but Captain Cowper, the carpenter, and myself, were not allowed to go into her. The boat then proceeded towards the *Zephyr*, with Mr. Lumsden and the captain of the corsair, and shortly after returned with some of the men whom the pirate had put on board; who brought with them Captain Cowper's watch, the ship's spy-glass, and my telescope, together with some of my clothes, and a goat. The goat had no sooner reached the deck, than one of these inhuman wretches cut its throat, and proceeded to flay it while it was yet alive, telling us at the same time, that we should all be served in the same manner if no money was found on board. The corsair had then got into four fathoms water and came to an anchor, as also did the *Zephyr*, about fifty yards from her, and the pirates that were on board began hailing their companions, & congratulating one another at their success.

The watch on board the corsair was now set, and Captain Cowper, the carpenter, and myself, were ordered to sleep on the Companion. Thither we repaired; but to sleep was impossible. The carpenter then took an opportunity of informing us that there was specie on board, and expressed his apprehension, that, if discovered, the cruel threat would be put into execution. Captain Cowper and myself, however, were ignorant of the circumstance, and felt rather inclined to believe that the carpenter was mistaken; but he assured us that such was the case, and that Mr. Lumsden had consulted him a day or two before about a place for its concealment. The expression which had dropped from him in the boat then occurred to us; but we still felt inclined to believe that it was some private money of his own. The whole night was passed in giving way to various conjectures, and hope and fear and the dread of assassination completely drove sleep away. Each reflected on what might be his future fate, and imparted his hopes or his apprehensions to his fellow-sufferers.

At daylight we perceived the pirates on board beating the *Zephyr's* crew with their cutlasses, & began to tremble for our own safety. After this we perceived the sailors at work hoisting out her boats, and hauling a rope cable from the after-hatchway and coiling it on deck, as if preparing to take out the brig's cargo. The crew of the corsair meanwhile began to take their coffee, and the officers invited us to partake of some, which we willingly did, & found it very refreshing after a night spent in sleepless apprehension.

At seven o'clock the Captain hailed his crew from the *Zephyr*, where he had passed the night, and ordered the boat to be sent, in which he returned in a short time, with some curiosities belonging to myself. On his arrival, he approached me, and, brandishing a cutlass over my head, told me to go on board the *Zephyr*, & bring every thing necessary for the purposes

11

of navigation, as it was his determination to keep me. To this mandate I made no reply; so, brandishing his cutlass again, he asked me, with an oath, if I heard him. I replied that I did, when, with a ferocious air, he said, 'Mind and obey me then, or I will take off your skin.' At this threat I went into the boat, and pulled towards the *Zephyr*, and on my arrival found Mr. Lumsden at the gangway. I told him the nature of my visit, at which he expressed his sorrow, but advised me not to oppose the pirate, lest it might produce bad usage, as he seemed bent upon detaining me. He then informed me that they had taken possession of every thing, and that he himself had narrowly escaped assassination on account of his watch.

On entering my cabin, I found my chest broken to pieces, & its contents taken away, with two diamond rings and some articles of value. From a seaman I received my gold watch, sextant, and some other valuable things, which I had previously given to him to conceal; and with these I returned to my own state-room, & proceeded to pack up what few clothes had been left by the plunderers. My books, parrot, and various other articles, I gave in charge to Mr. Lumsden, who engaged to deliver them safely into the hands of my friends, should he reach England.

The corsair had, during the interim, weighed anchor and hauled alongside of the *Zephyr*; and, having made fast, the crew had commenced moving all the trunks on board of her. Among these was the desk of Captain Cowper, containing all his papers and vouchers, which he begged me to claim as mine and recover for him, for which purpose he gave me the key. Well aware of the serious loss he would sustain, I undertook the dangerous task; and, passing into the corsair, informed the captain that my desk had been taken, and begged, as it only contained papers, which were of importance to my family, that it might be restored. He ordered me to open it, and, having examined the interior, he granted my request; and I had the pleasure of obliging Captain Cowper, who, in return, promised to represent my case to the underwriters at Lloyd's.

The pirates next commenced taking out the *Zephyr's* cargo, at which Mr. Lumsden & myself were compelled to assist; but the former was soon after removed on board the schooner, in consequence of the crying of the children, who, the captain said, had been instigated by him to do so. There he was employed in striking the cargo into the hatchways. The pirates in the mean time became intoxicated, and gave way to the most violent excesses. All subordination was at an end, and equality seemed to be the order of the day. Mr. Lumsden was now called on board the *Zephyr*, and questioned as to the cargo down the main hatchway, when he read & explained the manifesto. Orders were immediately given to four sailors and myself to prepare for hoisting the cargo up, and to clear away the dye wood that was in our way. Mr. Lumsden directed us to throw it overboard, which we commenced doing, and threw some over; but this was prevented by the Captain, who said that he only wanted to throw the ship's cargo overboard, in order to say that it was taken from him, and defraud the underwriters. We continued our occupation until we had hoisted up two scroons of indigo, a quantity of arrow root, and as much coffee as they thought sufficient. The seamen were then ordered to send down the fore-top gallant mast and yard, both of which were taken on board the pirate, with whatever spars they thought would be of utility.

Even the playful innocence of the children could not protect them from the barbarity of these ruffians; their ear-rings were taken out of their ears, and they were left without a bed to lie upon or a blanket to cover them.

They next commenced taking out the ship's stores, with all the live stock and some water; and Mr. Lumsden and Captain Cowper were then ordered on the quarter deck, and told that if they did not either produce the money or tell where it was concealed, the *Zephyr* should be burned and they with her. On this occasion the same answer was given as before, and the inhuman wretch instantly prepared to put his threat into execution, by sending the children on board the schooner, and ordering those two gentlemen to be taken below decks and to be locked to the pumps. The mandate was no sooner issued than it was obeyed by his fiendlike myrmidons, who even commenced piling combustibles round them. The apparent certainty of their fate extorted a confession from Lumsden, who was released and taken on deck, where he went to the round house and produced a small box of doubloons, which the pirate exhibited with an air of exultation to the crew. He then insisted that there was more; and, notwithstanding that the other made the most solemn asseverations to the contrary, and that even what he had given was not his own, he was again lashed to the pumps. The question was then applied to Captain Cowper, and fire was ordered to be put to the combustibles piled round him. Seeing his fate inevitable, he offered to surrender all he had, and, being released, he gave them about nine doubloons, declaring that what he had produced was all he had, and had been entrusted to his care for a poor woman, who, for aught he knew, might at this moment be in a state of starvation. 'Do not speak to me of poor people,' exclaimed the fiend, 'I am poor, and your Countrymen and the Americans have made me so; I know there is more money, and will either have it, or burn you and the vessel.' The unfortunate man was then once more ordered below, and fire directed to be applied. In vain did they protest that he had got all; he persisted in his cruelty. The flames now began to approach their persons, and their cries were heart-rending, while they implored him to turn them adrift in a boat, at the mercy of the waves rather than torture them thus, and keep the *Zephyr*, when, if there was money, he would surely find it.

Finding that no further confession was extorted, he began to believe the truth of these protestations, & ordered his men to throw water below and quench the flames. The unfortunate sufferers were then released and taken into the round house, and the seamen, children, and myself, allowed to go on board the brig. There we were left for a while at liberty, while the pirates caroused and exulted over their booty.

When they had finished their meal, the captain told them that it was now time to return to their own vessel, and ordered me to accompany them. I hesitated at first to obey; but he was not to be thwarted, and, drawing his knife, threatened with an oath to cut my head off if I did not move instanter. I thought it best to pretend ignorance of his order, and said that I had not heard him at first, and hoped, as I had some accounts to settle with Mr. Lumsden, that he would give me time to do so before he took me away.

He complied, with some difficulty. I then requested Mr. Lumsden to sign a written bill of lading for the two tierces of coffee belonging to me on board, consigned to Mr. Watson, ship-chandler, in London, and also a promissory note for eighteen pounds ten shillings, payable to the same person, on account of monies due to me.

Having made these arrangements, I returned on board the schooner, and the captain asked me if I had my watch. I answered in the affirmative; he took it from me and looked at it, and, admiring it, gave very strong hints that he should like to have it. I took no notice of the hint, and said that it was a gift from my aged mother, whom I never expected to see again, and should like to send it to her by Mr. Lumsden; but I was afraid that his people would take it away from that person, if I gave it into his hands. 'Your people have a very bad opinion of us,' he replied; 'but I will convince you that we are not so bad as we are represented to be; come along with me, and your watch shall go safely home.' Saying this, he took me on board the *Zephyr*, with the watch in his hand, and gave it to Mr. Lumsden, and desired his people not to take it from him on any account. I then asked to remain awhile, & bid farewell to the children and crew; which he, with some difficulty, allowed me to do. In this interval, the owner's son, who was on board learning navigation, said that his quadrant and all his clothes had been taken away, and begged me to recover them for him, if possible. I promised him I would do my best, and represented to the pirate that he was the son of poor parents, and could ill afford the loss, and begged that they might be restored. He sulkily replied, that I was presuming too much, but this must be my last request; and the lad might have his things, with the exception of checked shirts, which must be left for his crew. Having performed this good office, the captain became impatient for my return, and I was obliged to take a hasty but affecting leave of my former mess-mates, to become one of a desperate banditti. The inhuman wretch thought even this affecting ceremony too long, and drove me on board at the point of his knife.

When I had reached the deck of the corsair, he asked me if I had got every instrument necessary to the purposes of navigation; and if not, to go and get them, for he would have no excuses by and by, and if I made any he would kill me. I answered, that I had got all that was necessary, and he then gave orders to cast loose from the *Zephyr*, and told Mr. Lumsden he might proceed on his voyage, but on no account to steer for the Havannah; for, if he overtook him on that course, he would destroy him and his vessel together.

He promised that he would not touch there, and the vessels were accordingly cast loose, in a short time afterwards. Mr. Lumsden, Captain Cowper, & the children, stood on the gangway and bade me adieu, and my heart sunk within me as the two vessels parted.

The horrors of my situation now rushed upon my mind; I looked upon myself as a wretch, upon whom the world was closed for ever: exposed to the brutality of a ferocious and remorseless horde of miscreants – doomed to destruction and death, and, perhaps, to worse, to disgrace and ignominy; to become the partaker of their enormities, and be compelled, I knew not how soon, to embrue my hands in the blood of a fellow-creature, and, perhaps, a fellow-countryman. The distraction, grief, and painful apprehensions of my parents, and of one to whom I was under the tenderest of all engagements, filled my mind with terror. I could no longer bear to look upon the scene my fancy presented to me, and I would have sought a refuge from my own miserable thoughts, in self-destruction; but my movements were watched, and I was secured, and a guard set over me. The captain then addressed me, and told me that if I made a second attempt I should be lashed to a gun, and there left to die through hunger; and, for the sake of security, ordered me below; but, at my earnest entreaty, I was allowed to remain on deck till it was dark.

The *Zephyr* had got under weigh, and had set her sails; but I could perceive that her boats had either been cut or set adrift. This did not escape the notice of the pirate, who called to me, and said, 'Look at that rascal, he has cut loose his old boats, and when he gets home he will say that I have taken them, and get new ones from the underwriters; but I will write to Lloyd's, and prevent it.' He then appeared very anxious to know whether I thought they would go to the Havannah; of which he seemed so apprehensive, that he would have gone after the *Zephyr* and destroyed her, had I not said that they would in all probability pursue a direct course.

The wind was light, & the sea calm, but the weather was thick and heavy. Both vessels moved slowly through the water from one another, and I kept my eyes upon the *Zephyr* as long as she was visible, and then gave way to melancholy reflections on my forlorn and wretched condition. At dusk we anchored at the edge of the reef, and a boat was despatched to the shore, to inform the inhabitants of their good success. At daylight, the pirate stood to the south-west, &, at nine o'clock in the morning, entered a delightful harbour, where she anchored in two fathoms of water.

This harbour, called by the Spaniards Rio Medias, is large, commodious, and capable of containing a hundred sail. The anchorage is good, being a com pound of clay and mud; and it is protected from every wind except the north. Vessels within it ride very safe and easy, as the reef breaks off the force of the sea. The distance of it is about three miles from the edge of the reef to the southward, and the entrance intricate and hazardous. At two o'clock in the afternoon, I perceived a number of boats and canoes pulling towards the corsair and the captain told me that he expected a great deal of company from the shore, and, among others, two or three magistrates and their families, and some priests, observing also that I should see several pretty Spanish girls. I remarked, that I wondered he was not afraid of the magistrates.

He laughed, and said I did not know the Spanish character. Presents of coffee and other little things, said he, will always ensure their friendship; and from them I receive intelligence of all that occurs at the Havannah, and know every hostile measure time enough to guard against it.

Two magistrates, a priest, and several ladies and gentlemen now came on board, and were received in great pomp by the captain, whom they congratulated on his success. I was then introduced to them, as a captive, detained to navigate the vessel, and underwent much questioning from all of them, as to my country, and whether I came from London, and of what religion I was. Refreshments were then introduced, and the whole party drank the captain's health. Dancing was then proposed by the females, and preparations made for it. The parties stood up for their favourite amusement, and, to my great annoyance, I was selected as a partner for one of the magistrate's daughters. I declined the honor that was intended me, rather abruptly; but the young lady herself, notwithstanding my apparent rudeness, pressed me to know the cause of my refusal. I told her, candidly, that my thoughts were too much occupied by my melancholy situation, & the misery which it would occasion my wife and family, to take any interest in the amusement. 'You cannot be a married man,' replied she, with an air of naïveté, 'for I have been told, that when people are married, they always endeavour to conceal it.' I repeated that I was, and she appealed to the captain, who replied, that I had told him so, but he did not believe it, as Mr. Lumsden had assured him to the contrary. She said that she had heard a great deal of the gallantry of my countrymen, but she had never seen one of them until now. I hoped, I replied, that she would not form an unfavourable opinion of them from my want of it; but that my mind was so agitated, and my spirits so depressed, that I must entreat her to excuse my not accepting the high honor that was intended me, by selecting me as her partner. She said, with a look that clearly indicated that she felt as she spoke, that she sincerely pitied me, and felt deeply interested in my behalf; and that if it was possible for her, either to alleviate my sufferings, or to procure my liberty, she should be happy in doing so, and would endeavour to persuade her father to exert his influence, and have me released. I beseeched her not to be rash in her application; for, if the captain should discover that I was endeavouring secretly to interest either her or her father in my behalf, it might cost me my life. Our conversation was here interrupted by the captain, who, seeing that we did not join the dancers, asked the cause; and, on being informed, roughly ordered me to lead the young lady out immediately – a mandate that I did not dare to disobey.

As I shall have occasion to mention this young lady very often in the course of this narrative, it may be as well for me here to give some description of her. Her Christian name I afterwards discovered to be Seraphina, by which I shall hereafter designate her; her family name I never knew. She was young, and evidently unacquainted with the world, and therefore ignorant of the artifices practised in it. She was unembarrassed in her manners, and there was an openness and frankness in all that she said or did, that, under any other circumstances, might, perhaps, have had a more powerful influence. Her features were regular and pretty, but not handsome; and her eyes sparkling, animated, and full of intelligence. She was a brunette, and her whole appearance was of that description which interests the beholder, almost at first sight. In her disposition she was kind, benevolent, and humane, and possessed of strong and warm feelings, which were very manifest when she was interested in any thing.

During the dance, I could plainly perceive that she was hurt at the arbitrary conduct of the captain, and she very soon pleaded indisposition, and sat down. The instant the attention of the party was diverted from her, she regretted, in a mournful tone of voice, the unpleasant sensations of which she must have been the cause; and then, as if rallying her spirits, passed on to indifferent subjects, and made many inquiries into our manners and customs; asking me if all the stories she had heard of the grandeur and riches of London were true, & what sort of a building the immense church was that every body went to see. The manner in which she entered into conversation, and the very great degree of feeling and interest that she betrayed on my account, led me to flatter myself that I had made some tender impressions on her heart. Pity, I had heard say, was akin to love, & methought if I should be happy enough to inspire her with the latter passion, she might become instrumental in my escape. My opinion, however, of the Spanish character was not very high. I suspected treachery might lurk beneath this apparent warmth of feeling, and was determined to meet stratagem by stratagem, if such should be the case. I hinted, therefore, that my holding her so long in conversation, might give offence to her father, as I was an utter stranger, and a mere captive. She replied, not at all, as he was an indulgent parent, and never interfered with her.

Having so far satisfied myself, I endeavoured to obtain some knowledge of the situation of the country, and what towns or villages were along the shore. This naturally led to the question, whether I should like to go on shore, and I replied in the affirmative, making a bad state of health as a plea for my wishes. She immediately volunteered to obtain me the pirate's permission to go there, and said she had a ready excuse, without implicating me in the application, which was – that most of the inhabitants had never seen an Englishman; and, my being allowed to go to the village, would be conferring a favour on them, and would gratify their curiosity.

The rest of the party were, at this time, engaged in the dance, and her father and the priest were enjoying their wine, which they praised as the finest they had ever tasted; all, therefore, had been too busily employed to have observed us. Seraphina now left my side, and went to the captain; and, in a few moments, I saw her in earnest conversation with him, & I easily guessed the subject of it. I saw that the result was not favourable, as she evidently left him chagrined, and then went to her father. After exchanging a few words with him, he rose, and accompanied her towards the captain. This mutual explanation raised my hopes, and, as she had before said that if permission was obtained a horse should be waiting on the beach to convey me to her father's house, I resolved to take advantage of that circumstance, to escape. But, alas! those hopes were ill-founded; she soon returned to inform me that the pirate was inexorable, and had positively denied the favour, although her father had promised to become responsible for my safety.

As the day was far spent, the visitors began to talk of returning, & the dance broke up. Refreshments of fowls and sweetmeats, which had been taken from the *Zephyr*, were then served up; but there was no want of knives, forks, or spoons, as on former occasions, as the pirates had secured those belonging to the brig. When they had refreshed themselves, the captain commenced the distribution of wines and other things, as presents to his guests. A trunk, belonging to me, that contained linen and silks, fell to the lot of the priest, who was highly pleased, and told the captain he might be assured of his prayers, and indeed ought to attribute his present success to the intercessions which he had made with the Virgin. All, indeed, appeared gratified with their treatment, and told the captain that they had sent information round the country, that the corsair had rums, sugars, and coffee, for sale; who replied, that if they meant to come and purchase, they must do so quickly, as he should go on a cruise in a day or two.

While the rest were thus engaged, Seraphina imparted to me the ill success of her mission, and said that the priest had also unwittingly joined in her request. She then assured me of her esteem, and her future exertions; promised to visit me often, and took leave of me. The party now took to their boats and canoes, and the priest, in descending, invited the captain to dine with him, and to be sure and bring me with him when he came.

As soon as the party had gone, the captain came to me, and enquired whether I had commissioned Seraphina to make the request. As I was prepared for this question, I immediately answered in the negative,

& added, that I could have no object in going on shore, as I was a stranger; and, as to escape, that was out of the question, as I was totally unacquainted with the face of the country. He then said, if I behaved well he would take me with him; & immediately turned the conversation on the influence which he possessed with the magistracy of the whole island, saying that he could obtain passes for himself and his crew at all times, to travel from one part to another. These passes, from what I could understand, are passports issued and signed by the different magistrates, without which, persons travelling are liable to be thrown into prison, unless they can give a good account of themselves.

The captain was at this time very much intoxicated, as was usually the case with him in the afternoon; and when in that state, was wantonly cruel. Something just then excited his brutal temper, and he hastily drew his knife, and told me to go down into the cabin, and not come on deck any more, and that I must in future lie on the bare floor. I pleaded my ill-health and begged a mattress; but he replied that he always slept on the deck himself, and I must do the same, nor would he have his cabin lumbered up. His usual berth was on deck at the cabin door, where also two or three of his officers slept; so that it was impossible for any person to go out without awaking them. I passed the whole of the night in meditating on the means of escape; but almost every plan was abandoned as impracticable as soon as it was formed.

In the morning, when the crew had breakfasted, and the decks had been washed, preparations were made for exposing their plunder for sale. About eleven o'clock, Seraphina and her father came, and after the usual compliments had passed between them and the captain, she came to me, shook me by the hand, seemed glad to see me, & remarked that I appeared in better spirits. She then informed me that her mother was very desirous of seeing me, and that her father had been prevailed upon to renew his application to the captain. I thought this a favourable opportunity to put my plan into execution, and told her how completely her kindness and benevolence had gained my heart, and that if ever I recovered my liberty, I should do all in my power to deserve her esteem. I then added, that I was not a married man, but had made use of that artifice to preserve my liberty; and as that had failed, I thought it useless to persist in the declaration any longer. She appeared highly pleased at the confession; and I should have pursued the conversation, and, in all probability, elicited her sentiments, but for the arrival of strangers.

The sale then commenced, and I was placed at the steelyards to weigh out the coffee to the purchasers. To this, however, they objected, as they suspected I would cheat them; but they had no alternative, as no one else understood the use of steelyards, and the captain having informed them that I was a captive, and bore no share in the profits, they were content to let the sale go on. The best coffee was sold for ten dollars per hundred weight, its supposed half-value at Havannah, and the inferior at a similar rate. I observed that the purchasers all brought sacks and bags with them, as precautionary measures to prevent detection & destroy every clue to the market in which it was purchased. Having weighed their several pro-portions, a gun was fired, when two schooners of a small size came out from the land, and, when within hail, were ordered to come alongside & take the coffee on board. Neither the captain nor any part of his crew understood arithmetic, so that my next task was to make out the several bills; and their amount having been paid, a large dinner was prepared from the stock taken from the *Zephyr*.

While these preparations were going on, the captain told me, in English, which the rest did not understand, to make a strong mixture of spiritous liquors, that would rapidly intoxicate, and bring it up after dinner as an English cordial. In the mean time he informed the company, that, after dinner, he should set up to auction all the wearing apparel he had taken in this prize. They had all made perfectly free with the wine taken from the *Zephyr*, & the captain then told me to bring up the pretended cordial, which I had made from a mixture of wine, rum, gin, brandy, and porter, and recommended it to his guests, who drank it greedily and praised it. Its intoxicating effects were soon visible, and the auction then commenced.

The different trunks were brought upon deck, one by one, and as the contents of one was disposed of, another was opened, in order that the good and the bad might be sold alike. My own shared the fate of the rest, and I was obliged to see them pass into the hands of strangers, without daring to claim them. The cordial now had its intended effect, and the state of intoxication in which they were, caused them to contest every article, and accordingly, enormous sums were bid for the most trifling.

The sale being finished, they returned to the bottle, which gave me an opportunity of conversing with Seraphina, to whom I gave so glowing a description of every thing in England, that she said she would give worlds to see it. I then told her, that, were I at liberty, I should be happy to devote myself to her services; nay, that could I escape and she would accompany me, I would, on my arrival, marry her.

This sudden declaration startled her, and I began to be very much alarmed, that I had by this imprudence destroyed the very foundation of the fabric that I was endeavouring to erect, and the more so when, with an air of unusually cold solemnity, she replied, that I ought to remember that I was a stranger and a foreigner, and therefore it would be highly imprudent and improper for her to trust herself to my protection, and, what was still more important, that it would be the height of ingratitude to quit, in a clandestine manner, the roof of such indulgent parents as hers. I acquiesced in the justice of these remarks, but at the same time used all the sophistry of which I was master, to persuade her to think otherwise. To all my arguments she observed in reply, that should she consent to elope with me, a thousand obstacles must be surmounted before it could take place. The lower order of Spaniards were avaricious and treacherous, and would commit any crime for the sake of money, & therefore could not be trusted; to traverse the immense forests without a guide, was impossible; for to attempt it we should expose ourselves to destruction by wild beasts or starvation, and how to procure one that was trustworthy, she knew not. I was glad to hear her talk in this manner, for I began to hope my arguments had had some effect, nor was I mistaken. After some further doubts and fears, she promised to consider and inquire on the subject, and if she found it practicable, she would consent to escape with me to the Havannah, and thence to England. This promise overjoyed me, and I began to be sanguine in my hopes of escape.

What the cordial had begun, additional quantities of wine had completed; the whole party were very much intoxicated, and universal disorder prevailed. A quarrel took place between two of the crew, and a desperate fight with knives ensued, of which the rest were cool spectators. The battle was for a long time doubtful, as both fought with equal skill and an equal degree of caution, notwithstanding they were intoxicated, until one fell with a severe stab in the left breast, bleeding profusely. I was instantly called to administer to the wounded man; and it was in vain for me to declare that I knew nothing of the healing art. The captain swore at me, and said he knew to the contrary; for the master of the *Zephyr* had informed him that I had cured and saved the life of his sailmaker, who had fallen down the hold; and therefore if I did not cure him, he would serve me in the same manner. I saw it would be useless to make any reply; and therefore, having procured bandages, I staunched the blood and dressed his wounds in the best manner I was able. Having attended to one patient, I was then obliged to turn my attention to his antagonist, who had not escaped unhurt. When I had completed my task, I was carelessly complimented on my skill, and asked if the wound was mortal; which question I evaded, by saying I hoped not.

This brutal exhibition rendered me quite melancholy; and while I was standing lost in thought, Seraphina came up to me, and asked the reason; I told her, and added that such ruffianly conduct was not suffered in England. She said it was the custom of the country, and therefore I should not mind it. She then told me that she had been considering the subject of our conversation, and thought that it might be feasible, and was therefore determined to effect my liberation on the first favourable opportunity. Having thus raised my hopes, she went to her father, who was, like the rest of the party, much intoxicated, and tried to prevail on him to return; and, after considerable difficulty, succeeded in her wishes. This was a signal to the rest, and a general preparation for departure was the consequence. The schooners that had removed the coffee, had already taken leave of us, and the boats and canoes of the party were now brought round, and they all rowed off, Seraphina taking a very affectionate leave of me.

The guests were scarcely gone, when the captain went below and enquired of the least injured of the wounded men, the cause of their quarrel. He hesitated at first to tell, and supplicated that he might be forgiven for his neglect in not having furnished him with the important intelligence before. This being granted, he told the pirate that his antagonist was one of the party formed by the chief mate to assassinate him and the whole crew, and take possession of the ship and plunder. That officer, he informed him, had gone to the Havannah for the express purpose of bringing some more men, & that they were to put the plan into effect when himself and the crew were either asleep or inebriated. I saw that his brutal temper was excited by this information; his eyes flashed fire, and his whole countenance was distorted. He vowed destruction against the whole party, and, rushing upon deck, assembled the crew, and imparted what he had heard. The air rang with the most dreadful imprecations; they simultaneously rushed below and dragged the helpless wounded wretch upon deck, and, without taking into consideration that the accusation against him might be unfounded, proceeded to cut off his legs and arms with a blunt hatchet, then mangling his body with their knives, threw the yet warm corpse overboard. Not contented with having destroyed their victim, they next sated their vengeance on his clothes, and every thing belonging to him, which they cut in pieces and threw into the sea. Having glutted their vengeance in this summary manner, they went below & questioned the informer as to his accomplices; but he told them that the murdered man was the only one of the conspirators on board; that he had been persuading him to join them, and on his threatening to reveal the plot, had taunted him with cowardice, struck him, and provoked the quarrel, in order to put him out of the way. The ruffians seemed satisfied with this answer, and the captain told me to pay particular attention to his wounds, and cure him as fast as possible.

This dreadful scene threw a damp over my spirits, all hope of escape left me, and I looked upon every hour as my last; for I knew not how soon I might undergo the same fate. I determined, however, to be upon my guard, and by a ready compliance in every thing, prolong my existence, until Seraphina should have an opportunity of proving the sincerity of her promise.

When his fury had subsided, the captain asked me what I thought of the Spanish mode of fighting and, added, that I must learn the use of the knife observing that it was the first thing his father had taught him. He then told me, that if ever I knew or heard of any thing inimical to himself or his crew going on, and did not give him information, I should undergo the same fate as the man whom they had just punished for his perfidy. The watch was then set, the crew sharpened their knives as if preparing for attack, and I was ordered down below for the night.

The night passed off quietly, and in the morning I was directed to bend a new fore-top-sail. Every preparation was then made to go outside the reef. About noon a sail was discovered, and I was ordered aloft to examine, and report what description of vessel she was. When I had looked at her through my spy-glass, I gave notice that it was a schooner standing westward. The captain asked me if she was a merchant or a man of war, and added, 'mind you do not deceive me, for if you do, I will cut off your head. I have already killed several of your countrymen, and take care you do not add yourself to the number.' This threat made me apprehensive, and I was determined to examine her closely before I reported; and having done so, told him she was a merchantman.

The pirate was already under weigh, and she gave chase immediately. I was still at the mast-head, and could perceive that the schooner was aware of our intention, &, suspecting us to be a pirate, was altering her course and standing to the north. I informed him of this circumstance; and he abused me for not doing so sooner. When we had passed through the channels, and were without the reef, the wind died away, and the captain ordered out the sweeps, and the corsair made great way through the water. The breeze, however, soon freshened, and both vessels stood on under a press of sail. Before dark we were gaining rapidly upon her, but she was still at a great distance, and the captain despaired of reaching her, expressing his apprehension that she would escape, as she would most certainly alter her course in the night.

At ten o'clock at night she was out of view, and I was then ordered below. The captain declared, however, that he would stand on that tack until two in the morning, & if she was not then visible he would alter his course to the east. The fatigue I had undergone by being tossed to and fro in the tops made me sleep soundly, and I did not awake till called in the morning. When I came on deck I found all at a loss to know whereabouts they were. The whole crew had been intoxicated, no light had been in the binnacle, and no log had been thrown; no one therefore knew what the ship had been doing through the night, or what sail had been set. In this dilemma I was called upon to give the captain information as to the bearings of the harbour from which we had sailed the preceding day. I replied that it was impossible for me to inform him exactly, and was threatened with instant massacre if I did not. I then informed him if he would wait till noon I would endeavour to do so; and the same threat was repeated in case of failure.

It was a fortunate event for me, that at this time the sun was in distance with the moon, & the sky being remarkably clear, the sea smooth, and the schooner making very little way, I had an opportunity, at about nine o'clock, to take a good lunar observation. After I had completed taking the sights, which I was compelled to do above, as no one on board understood navigation, I made my calculations, and at noon obtained the true latitude by a good observation of the sun's altitude. To my great astonishment I found that we were about twenty leagues to the W.N.W. of Cape Buonavesta, a distance of two hundred miles to the westward of where I had imagined we were. The moment the captain perceived that I had finished operations, he asked the situation of the vessel, which I informed him; he then ordered me to direct the helmsman, and trim the sails according to the course which we ought to steer. Having obeyed this order, he asked me when we should see land, and I told him in the afternoon, if the breeze was favourable. He seemed to have some doubt, and declared, with an oath, he would punish me if we did not.

The breeze in the mean time freshened, and came more in our favour, & all appeared anxious to prove the truth of my information, and be convinced of my skill as a navigator: but no one was more anxious than myself or the least error in my calculation devoted me to destruction; and I trembled for the consequences. At four in the afternoon, to my great joy, the men on the look-out called, Land! and the coast-pilot complimented me on my skill; but the captain only abused me. 'You rascal, you pretended not to know where the vessel was; but you see you cannot deceive me, and I would advise you not to attempt it.' The pilot remarked that the current must have been running very strong.

A very material error seems to exist in the charts, as well as the books of instructions, on the subject of this current. Those which I have seen agree in stating that it runs to the eastward; whereas I have frequently found it to run westward at the rate of three knots, off Cape Roman, the Bay of Honde, the Camaoeners, and at some distance from the land. Cape Buonavesta too is erroneously laid down as high and mountainous, whereas the land about it is not more than eighteen feet from the surface of the ocean; and that which is in general mistaken for it, lies a great way in the interior of the island, and six leagues to the eastward of the Cape. The Colorados, so little known, and so much dreaded by mariners, is also erroneously laid down; an error which frequently occasions a serious loss of lives & property.

The north side of this reef may be approached without the smallest danger in the thickest darkness, by the precautionary throw of the lead, as the soundings gradually decrease from the depth of fifty fathoms till you come into three: but frequently there is no dependence to be placed upon it; for, at the distance of six yards, there may not be more than three feet of water. Within the reef are a number of fine bays and inlets, capable of containing a large fleet. The whole coast indeed abounds with bays, creeks, and inlets, little known to European navigators, that seem as if formed by nature for the reception and protection of those sanguinary hordes. While I had the misfortune of being among those miscreants, I have been, in several instances, in those places, within musket-shot of British and American men of war, & could plainly perceive the men in their tops from the mast-head of the corsair, without being perceived by them; the vessel being completely screened from observation by the trees. The coast pilot on board the corsair had certainly a very intimate knowledge of the whole coast, and knew every bay and inlet in it; and indeed boasted that that knowledge had for years been their protection, and assisted them in their depredations. Some had, according to their own confession, been seven or eight years at this lawless occupation.

The corsair pursued her course along the land to the eastward till dusk, and then cast anchor. At daylight on the following morning she again made sail for the harbour, which she did not reach till eleven, in consequence of the lightness of the wind. In the afternoon a boat full of men appeared coming towards the schooner, which, upon examination, was found to contain some of the chief mate's party. No sooner was this known than the captain declared he would kill them all, and ordered thirty muskets to be loaded and brought on deck. When the boat was about two hundred yards from the schooner, the men ceased rowing, and held up a white handkerchief for a signal, as if doubtful of their safety, which was answered by a similar one from on board, and they again advanced. When within reach of the musketry, the dreadful order of 'fire' was given. Five of the men fell in the boat, the sixth leaped over and began to swim, after whom a boat was despatched. On his being brought on board, the captain told him the accusation that was against him and his party, and threatened him with a cruel and lingering death, if he did not confess the whole truth. In vain did he declare his innocence, and ignorance of any plot; the ruffian was resolved to glut his vengeance, and ordered him to be stripped and exposed, naked, wounded, and bleeding as he was, to the scorching fervour of a July sun; the July sun of a tropical climate!

The feelings of humanity got the better of my caution, and I entreated the captain not to torture the poor wretch in that dreadful manner, declaring that I firmly believed him innocent; for, had he been guilty, torture and terror would have wrung a confession from him. In vain I pleaded, in vain I represented the inhumanity of punishing a poor wretch, in all probability innocent of the crime laid to his charge. He was deaf to my entreaties, & threatened me with vengeance for my interference, declaring that he had not done half that he intended to do.

Having said this, he turned to the man, told him that he should be killed, and therefore advised him to prepare for death, or confess himself to any of the crew whom I chose to call aside for that purpose.

The man persisted in his plea of innocence, declared that he had nothing to confess, and entreated them all to spare his life. They paid no attention to his assertions, but, by the order of the captain, the man was put into the boat, pinioned, and lashed in the stern, and five of the crew were directed to arm themselves with pistols and muskets and to go in her. The captain then ordered me to go with them, savagely remarking that I should now see how he punished such rascals, and giving directions to the boat's crew to

row for three hours backwards and forwards through a
narrow creek formed by a desert island and the island
of Cuba. 'I will see,' cried he, exultingly, 'whether the
musquitoes & the sandflies will not make him confess.'
Prior to our leaving the schooner, the thermometer was
above ninety degrees in the shade, and the poor wretch
was now exposed naked to the full heat of the sun. In
this state we took him to the channel, one side of
which was bordered by swamps full of mangrove
trees, and swarming with the venomous insects
before mentioned.

We had scarcely been half an hour in this place
when the miserable victim was distracted with pain;
his body began to swell, and he appeared one complete
blister from head to foot. Often in the agony of his torments did he implore them to end his existence and
release him from his misery; but the inhuman
wretches only imitated his cries, and mocked and
laughed at him. In a very short time, from the effects
of the solar heat and the stings of the musquitoes and
sandflies, his face had become so swollen that not a
feature was distinguishable; his voice began to fail, &
his articulation was no longer distinct.

I had long suspected that the whole story of the
conspiracy was a wicked and artful fabrication; and the
constancy with which this unfortunate being underwent these tortures, served to confirm my suspicions.
I resolved, therefore, to hazard my interference, and,
after much entreaty and persuasion, prevailed upon
them to endeavour to mitigate his sufferings, and to
let the poor wretch die in peace, as the injuries which
he had already sustained were sufficient of themselves to occasion death. At first they hesitated; but,
after consulting for some time among themselves,

they consented to go to the other side of the island where they would be secured from observation, and untie him and put something over him. When we had reached that place, we lay upon our oars and set him loose; but the moment he felt the fresh sea breeze, he fainted away. His appearance at this time was no longer human, and my heart bled at seeing a fellow creature thus tormented. When our time was expired, we again tied him as before, to prevent the fury of the Captain for our lenity, and once more pulled for the passage on our way to the vessel. On our arrival, his appearance was the source of merriment to all on board; and the captain asked if he had made any confession. An answer in the negative gave him evident disappointment, and he enquired of me whether I could cure him. I told him he was dying; 'then he shall have some more of it before he dies,' cried the monster, and directed the boat to be moored within musquet shot in the bay. This having been done, he ordered six of the crew to fire at him. The man fell, and the boat was ordered along-side. The poor wretch had only fainted; and when they perceived that he breathed, a pig of iron was fastened round his neck, & he was thrown into the sea. Thus ended a tragedy, which, for the miseries inflicted on the victim, and for the wanton and barbarous depravity of his fiend-like tormenters, never, perhaps, had its equal.

The inhuman wretches who had been the chief participaters in this horrid deed, seemed to regard it as an everyday occurrence: the guitar tinkled and the song went round, as if nothing had happened; and the torments which their victim had just undergone, and the cries that he had uttered, seemed to form the subject of their jests, and to be echoed in their barbarous mirth.

At nine o'clock at night I was ordered below, as usual; but the image of what had occurred haunted my slumbers, and my sleep was broken by constant apprehensions of assassination. Morning brought round my appointed task of attending the sick; after which I was ordered to make a new gaff top-sail. I went aloft and took the measure of the sail, and then informed the captain that it would be necessary to take the canvas on shore to cut it out. The very mention of the shore excited his fury, & he immediately accused me of intending to escape, observing that any endeavour would be fruitless, as he could have me apprehended in less than two hours after I should go. I told him I had merely said so with a view of expediting the work, and then proceeded to cut out the canvas upon deck in the best manner I could, using all diligence in making the sail. My exertions seemed to please him, and he frequently addressed me in a cheerful manner. Our attention was now excited by a cry of 'a sail, a sail,' from the mast-head, and I was driven up aloft with the usual threat, to reconnoitre, while the vessel got under weigh. I informed them that she was a merchant brig, and orders were given to go in chase immediately; the pilot undertaking to take her through the channels, while I was called down and consulted as to the best mode of fighting in case she should resist. The corsair having gained on the brig, fired a gun, and hoisted Spanish colours, which the other answered by heaving to and displaying the English ensign. From the painted ports and figure-head of the brig, the pirate began to suspect that she was a man of war, and was fearful of approaching any nearer; he therefore ordered the fore-top-sail to be laid aback, and said that he should send the boat to board her under my directions.

This intimation greatly alarmed me, and I pointed out to him the perils I should run in obeying his orders, and that, should I be captured hereafter, I should assuredly suffer an ignominious death. 'And what are you, sir,' cried he ferociously, 'that you should not suffer as well as myself? The schooner shall never be captured; for when I can no longer defend her, I shall blow her up: if you do not instantly go, I will shoot you.' I told him that he might shoot me if he pleased; but that I would not commit an act that might subject me and my family to disgrace. Seeing me resolute, and inclined to dispute his authority, he ordered his crew to blindfold me and carry me forward, and told me to prepare myself for death. I was carried as he had directed, and he then came to me, and asked me if I was prepared; I answered firmly, 'yes.' He then left me, and immediately a volley of musquetry was fired, but, evidently, only with a view to frighten me. The captain immediately came up to me, and asked if I was not desperately wounded? I answered, I was not; but begged if it was his intention to destroy me, to do it at once, and not trifle with me, as I preferred death to disgrace and ignominy. He then gave directions that I should be taken and lashed to the main-mast, and the bandage removed from my eyes. This order was quickly obeyed by his myrmidons. As soon as I was fastened to the mast, the captain cut up a number of cartridges, and place the powder round me on the deck, with a train to it, and gave orders for the cook to light a match and send it aft. He then repeated his order, and asked if I would obey him; I persisted in my refusal, and, without any further hesitation, he communicated the fire to the powder. The explosion deprived me of my senses, and stunned me for the moment; but I soon recovered, to undergo the most horrid torture: the flames had caught my clothes, which were blazing round me, and my hands were so pinioned, that I could not relieve myself. I begged them, for God's sake, to despatch me at once; but they only laughed at me, and the captain tauntingly asked me if I would obey him now? The excruciating agony in which I was, extorted my acquiescence, and I was ordered to be released; but I fainted before that could be done.

When I recovered my senses, I found myself stretched on a mattress in the cabin, and in the most dreadful pain. In the frenzy and delirium of the moment, I meditated self-destruction; but no weapons were near me, and the shattered state of my legs did not allow me to seek any. The steward was below, and I begged him to lend me his knife; but he suspected my intention, and informed the captain, who descended in a fury. 'You want to kill yourself, young man, I understand,' cried he; 'but I do not mean that you should die yet; I shall blow you up again, for I see it is the only way to make you obey me.' He then ordered them to keep watch over me, and help me to sit up and dress my wounds. I found my legs dreadfully injured, the flesh lacerated, and the bone in some parts laid bare; and by this time, large blisters had risen on various parts of my body. I asked for a sheet to cover me, and a pillow for my head; and the captain, who now seemed to relent, ordered the steward to give me all that I required. I begged that the medicine chest might be placed near me, which they did, & I seized that opportunity of swallowing the contents of a small vial of laudanum, about a hundred and thirty drops, hoping that I should wake no more in this world.

The cook, who seemed to pity and feel for my sufferings, now brought me a little arrow-root and wine, and made up my bed for me. I asked him where the corsair was, and he told me in the harbour at anchor. I expressed my surprise at the circumstance; when he informed me the captain was so convinced that the brig was a man of war, and that I had meant to decoy them to be taken, that he was afraid to attack, and had returned into harbour shortly after I was brought down below.

From this poor fellow I received a great deal of kindness, and he seemed possessed of much humanity. 'The captain,' said he, bending over me with a look of compassion, 'is a very bad man, and has killed more than twenty people with his own hand, in cool blood; and he would kill you too, were he not in want of your services.' He then cautioned me to appear cheerful and satisfied at all times, and that then they would treat me well: he also told me that he would prepare any little thing for me that I might want, and attend me by day and by night; and, with this kind assurance, left me to my repose.

I now began to feel the soporiferous effects of the laudanum, and, laying myself down upon my mattress, commended my soul into the hands of the God who gave it, beseeching him to forgive me for the act I had committed, and resigned myself, as I thought into the arms of death. I soon fell into a profound sleep, which lasted the whole night, and in the morning they found such difficulty to arouse me, that they imagined I had poisoned myself and was dead.

The captain accused me of having done so, and threatened me with a second torturing if I ever made another attempt. I told him I had merely taken some opiate medicine to render me insensible to the pain I suffered, and that it had taken an unusually powerful effect upon me. He then asked me if I could attend to the sick? I said that I would endeavour to do so; but, upon attempting to rise, I found my strength fail, and my limbs so stiff and in such a state, that I began to think that I had lost their use. A mattress was however placed under me to help me to sit up, & the medicine chest placed by my side; and in this manner, although it put me to excruciating agony, I began to perform my task.

Having attended to the sick, I next dressed my own wounds, which had assumed a dangerous appearance.

While thus occupied below, the master of a coasting schooner brought intelligence that the *Zephyr* had arrived at the Havannah, and that all the circumstances of her capture and plunder had been made known. Frantic at this information, he rushed into the cabin; 'see,' cried he, 'what dependence can be placed on your countrymen. That old rascal has gone to the Havannah, & broken a solemn promise. But for this I should not care, had he told the truth. He has told the authorities there that I have plundered him of specie to the amount of fifteen hundred pounds sterling, whereas I did not obtain half that amount. He has said also, that I maltreated the children; and he must have known that it was only on their account that I did not destroy the vessel, but allowed him to proceed on his voyage. But this will be a lesson to me not to trust the English again; for I now find them as treacherous as the Americans.' This he uttered all in a breath, and then paused as if considering something. A malignant scowl passed over his face, and he proceeded: 'He thinks he is out of my reach; but, mark me, if he remains a few days longer at the Havannah, he shall never live to see England. I have three or four already on the watch to assassinate him; they must be new to the trade, or it would have been done ere this: but there is one on board who will soon accomplish it; a man who has already despatched several; I shall send him there in an hour; and, to make sure of his performing it, I will give him ten doubloons for the deed. Nay, should he be fortunate enough to escape this time, I may take him again at some other; and then I will tie him to a tree in the forest, and let him starve.' During this conversation, the villain had been preparing himself, and now announced that he was ready to proceed on his sanguinary mission. The boat was then ordered to put him on shore, where he was to procure a horse & direct his course to the Havannah; and the savage entered it with an air of exultation, and with loud promises of his performing his task faithfully.

The hope of revenge seemed to have calmed his turbulence, and he began asking me how soon I should be able to proceed with the sail, and to go up aloft; adding, that my own foolish obstinacy had occasioned all my sufferings. I told him that I was very ill, and could not then attempt it; to which he coolly answered, that he was anxious to have the vessel completely fitted with new sails; and hoped that I should be able to do so very soon. He then turned about and left the cabin.

The whole schooner's company now went to their evening meal; and, as was usual, to drink, play the guitar, and carouse. Their merriment was, however, soon interrupted by the dashing of approaching oars. They instantly flew to quarters, and made every preparation for acting on the defensive; and I was dragged on deck, wounded as I was, to hail the boat in English. Immediately on my doing so, the boat stopped, and I repeated the hail, but they did not answer; upon which, the captain called to them in Spanish. His voice was soon recognized, and they came alongside. All were eager to learn the object of their visit, and rapid in their enquiries. They then informed the captain that a boat containing some more of the chief mate's party had arrived, and having heard of the fate of their associates, had vowed revenge; for this purpose, they had gone in pursuit of the man who had been just set on shore of whose arrival they were informed; and had, when they left, followed him towards the magistrate's house, where he had gone to procure a pass for his journey. They added, that if he wished to preserve the man's life, he must lose no time in sending him assistance.

A general panic seemed to have seized the whole crew at this intelligence, & no one seemed inclined to go upon this hazardous enterprise. The captain now upbraided, now threatened, and now abused them by turns, but with no visible effect; and was on the point of abandoning his emissary to his fate, when one man, apparently bolder than the rest, but evidently with hesitation, offered his services, and even declared his resolution to perish in the attempt.

This example had the desired effect, and nine more stepped forward. They were hastily supplied with arms and ammunition, and despatched on shore, strictly charged by the captain to give the assailants no quarter.

When this expedition was despatched, the pirate asked me whether, if I had been well, I would have volunteered to rescue Stromeda, for so the man was called. Wishing for an opportunity to lull his suspicions against me, I answered in the affirmative; adding, at the same time, that he ought to be on his guard, for this report might have been a stratagem to withdraw part of the crew, in order to attack the schooner more easily. The hint staggered him; he confessed the idea had never occurred to him, and thanked me for my precautionary advice; adding, 'I see now, that necessity is the best teacher, and I shall, at last, make something of you.'

I was then sent below again, and the captain proceeded to take measures to guard against surprise. A watch was set on deck, and every one lay down with his arms by his side. All was silence and watchful anxiety, till midnight, when the boat returned with only five of the men. These informed the captain, that, on the beach, they had met a servant despatched by the magistrate, who informed them that Stromeda was a prisoner, and that the captors had vowed to put him to death, and bade them hasten to his rescue. The party had, on hearing this, taken a circuitous rout through the wood; and, having eluded the scouts of the chief mate's gang, had surprised four of them playing at cards and drinking under a tree. Having secured these, they proceeded to the magistrate's residence, and, firing through the doors and windows, discharged their blunderbusses into the house, regardless of who might be within, whether friend or foe; and had, in so doing, unfortunately wounded the magistrate himself. Stromeda they

found bound hand and foot, lying on the floor; but, as
he had not been injured, and having loosed him, he
proceeded on his journey. Two of the chief mate's
party, they said, had been killed, two more were prisoners, and two who were acting as scouts, perceiving
what had happened, had escaped after firing their
musquets and wounding one of the corsair's crew.
They concluded this long narration with an earnest
request on the part of the magistrate and wounded
man, that I might be instantly despatched to dress
their wounds, as there was no medical man near them.
I was in consequence ordered to prepare for my new
task as quick as possible. In vain did I remonstrate on
the cruelty of the measure, and try to move their pity
by showing them the mangled and deplorable state in
which I was. I was told, in reply, that as much care as
possible should be taken not to hurt me in moving,
but that go I must. Seeing them resolved, I prepared
to comply; a mattress stretched on one of the hatches,

was placed in the boat, and I was lowered down upon it; and the party who had charge of me, having received orders to be careful and gentle in their usage, shoved off the boat, and rowed towards shore.

It was past two in the morning before we reached the shore, and landed close to a house, where we found a horse and a man in waiting for us. I was taken into the house while they formed a sort of a litter for me, with a bed fastened on the animal's back; upon this I was placed, & the party proceeded about two miles and a half through a forest, to the magistrate's residence; on our arrival at the door, I was taken off the litter, and the first object that met my view was Seraphina, who rushed into my arms, crying, 'for God's sake, take me, for they have just killed my father;' and burst into tears. The distress in which she was, made me conclude that he was dead; and when I was carried into a miserable apartment, meanly furnished, I was met by her mother, to whom Seraphina exclaimed, 'Oh, my dear mother, this is the good Englishman come to cure my father.' In the room, there were only two beds and a leather-bottomed chair. Upon one of the beds was stretched the magistrate, covered with blood, and on the other the wounded pirate. Being placed by the side of the former, I gave directions to have him stripped, and then proceeded to examine his wound. One ball had slightly fractured his left arm, and passed into the shoulder, and another had lodged in the arm. The latter, I easily extracted, and reduced the fracture in the best manner I was able, & bound up the wound. The wife and daughter remained silent, but anxious, spectators of my operations; and, when I had concluded, asked me if the old man would survive, to which I gave a favourable answer, & then dressed the wounds of the other sufferer. The house, while I was attending to the wounded man, was thronged with the villagers, part of whom had come from curiosity to see me, and part to inquire after their magistrate. During these operations, the pirates who had accompanied me, had been absent; but, on their return, they told me that they had been burying Pepe, one of their comrades, who had been killed in the rencontre. They had with them the two prisoners they had taken, bound hand and foot, and beside them, on the ground, were the bleeding corpses of the other two, mangled in a dreadful manner. One of these they threw across a horse, and, taking the two prisoners, they proceeded towards the beach, leaving four men to take care of me. The prisoners were fastened on each side of the horse to the dead body, &, in this manner, they marched in triumph through the village without being interfered with.

After they were gone, I was removed and placed on a bed in another room, where Seraphina came to me. When I had related to her how I had been reduced to my present miserable situation, I reminded her of her promise, and asked her if her sentiments had undergone any change. She replied, 'not at all;' but, while her father's life remained in a state of uncertainty, she could not bear the idea of leaving him, strong as her affection for me was; and besides, she added, 'in your present state you are unfit to perform so long and so fatiguing a journey.' I commended the first reason, and acquiesced in the last; and told her that I should, no doubt, be frequently sent ashore to attend to her father, who was in no real danger, & that a favourable opportunity might offer on one of those visits. I begged her, therefore, if she did really love me, to endeavour and make such preparations that we might be enabled to go at the shortest notice; adding, at the same time, that I had been robbed of all my money, and must depend upon her for finding the means for our journey. 'Do not let these considerations make you uneasy,' cried she, pressing my hand in the most affectionate manner, and smiling in my face; 'I have resolved to accompany you, and will remove every obstacle in the best way I can; but caution is necessary; and therefore you must learn to be patient, and not think me insincere because my movements do not keep pace with your wishes.'

The horses had now returned from conveying the prisoners, and the men, entering to inform me of their arrival, interrupted our conversation. I bade Seraphina adieu, and, with a light heart, suffered them to carry me to the litter, which was made the same as for merly. Before we set off, the magistrate sent word to beg that I might be allowed to visit him on the following day. The body of the other man was now fastened across one of the horses, and the party proceeded towards the beach.

When we arrived at the place where the boat was stationed, the dead body was cut from the horse, and flung into the sea. A line was then fastened to the neck, and attached to the boat, for the purpose of towing it into deep water, where they intended to sink it, and had brought a stone with them for that purpose. It was at this time broad daylight, and we had scarce rowed a hundred and fifty yards from the shore, when we perceived a man, closely pursued by the inhabitants, rush towards the shore, plunge into the sea, and swim after the boat. The crew pulled towards him, and took him in. On inquiry, he proved to be one of the chief mate's party, and they deliberately told him that he must die, pointing out to him, at the same time, the mangled body of his late associate. The poor wretch seeing that he had only escaped from one set of barbarians to fall into the hands of a worse, burst into an agony of tears, and implored them to have mercy on him. The inhabitants, in the mean time, demanded, with loud cries, that he should be delivered up, and the boat returned apparently for that purpose; but, after some altercation, they resolved to keep and murder him themselves, and again left the shore, with the determination to torture him in the swampy passage where they had already destroyed one victim. When they had arrived at the entrance of that pestiferous spot, they sunk the dead body, after inflicting some indignities upon it; & thence proceeded to strip their lately acquired prisoner, whom they lashed on the boat, gagged and pinioned, and pulled into the channel. The body of the miserable being was soon covered with musquitoes and sand-flies, and he writhed with the agony of their stings. In this state they carried him to where a tree projected into the waters, on which they placed him, blindfolded, shot him, and then made the best of their way to the corsair.

On their arrival, they exultingly told their companions of their cruelty, not only what I had witnessed, but what they had inflicted on the other two captives whom I had seen bound at the magistrate residence. These poor wretches they had fastened to trees, and fired at them as targets; and one monster boasted that he had lost a bet of a doubloon because he had not killed his man first.

Weak and fatigued as I was, from want of rest, I was ordered to attend to the sick on board. The wounded man I found was now quite well, and endeavoured to impress upon his mind that he owed his life entirely to my exertions, which he verily believed; for he declared that I should never want friend while he was on board. Having performed this office, I dressed my own wounds, which I found less painful, and assuming a more favourable aspect. The captain came in and examined them, and expressed a hope that I should soon be able to make the sail and go up aloft, which I told him I should be able to do in three or four days. He then questioned me on the subject of the magistrate's disaster and told me that I must pay every possible attention him, as he was a very worthy man, and his best friend. In order to lull his suspicions, I pretended unwillingness to go so frequently ashore, and recommended him to send for a medical man; but he over ruled my objections, and said that he was quite confident in my skills.

On this day he was perfectly sober, which was seldom the case, and he began to display a feeling of kindness towards me, remarked I must be fatigued, and recommended me to take a few hour's sleep – a recommendation that I willingly followed, and slept till I was called up to dinner. After dinner I tried to continue making the sail, with which he was highly pleased. I worked at it till near nine in the evening, when he told me that I had done enough and had better go to bed.

At five o'clock on the following morning, I resumed my labours, & by breakfast time had got the whole put together. After breakfast, I attended to the sick, as usual; and, in the mean time, the sail was hoisted up by the captain's desire, to see whether it would answer, and he expressed himself highly pleased with it. In the afternoon I was to visit the magistrate, but another event prevented me.

About eleven in the forenoon, there was a cry of 'a sail,' and, notwithstanding my wounds, I was ordered aloft to look out and examine. With great torture and much difficulty, I reached my post, and discovered a ship close hauled standing towards land, with her larboard tacks aboard, and having the appearance of a merchantman. The moment I gave this information the schooner was got under weigh, and proceeded in chase. The motion of the vessel now became extremely painful to me, and I came down on deck, which the captain no sooner perceived than he rushed up to me, and beat me over the head & shoulders with the flat part of a cutlass, exclaiming, 'When I was on board an English man of war, if I had come down without orders, I should have got six dozen lashes; and I will serve you as your countrymen served me.' I was then forced up aloft a second time, and might have suffered harsher usage, but for the interference of some of the officers, who interposed between us. In a few minutes, the ruffian followed me up, and told me to examine and tell him what vessel she was. I endeavoured to do so, as well as I could, and told him that it was a Dutch vessel, which he imparted to his crew, who gave three cheers. He himself was highly pleased at the intelligence, called me a good fellow, expressed his sorrow for mal-treating me, and said the Dutch vessels were good prizes, as they always carried specie to purchase their cargo. I thought this a good opportunity to get released from my painful situation, and asked his leave to go down on deck, which he granted me.

The Dutchman appeared suspicious of the corsair, and now endeavoured to bear away; but it was too late, for the pirate sailed very fast, and was nearly up to him. To decoy them, English colours were run up, and a gun fired, upon which they hauled up their main sail, and tacked towards the corsair. The captain suspected that they meant to resist, & therefore hauled his wind until the Dutchman was within reach of the long gun, which he fired at him, pulling down the English colours, and running up the red flag, at the same time. The shot struck close under his bows, and he instantly laid aback the main topsail. When we were within hail, I was ordered to hail her in English, and desire the captain to bring his papers on board. The Dutchman was rather slow in obeying the order, and a volley of musquetry was fired over their heads, which quickened their movements. When they came on board, they exhibited symptoms of the greatest terror, and their papers were taken from them, and given to me to examine. It was in vain for me to plead ignorance of their language, as I was compelled to know every thing; I therefore pretended to read them, and attempted to guess at their contents. The captain of the Dutchman was, in the mean time, interrogated as to what money he had on board, and the same threat held out to him that had been held out to the master of the *Zephyr*. The pirate then went on board the prize, with a pilot and four of his crew, leaving the Dutch captain a prisoner on board the schooner, and, immediately on his arrival, they made sail, and both vessels steered for the harbour, but were prevented, by the current, from beating into the channel, & anchored without the reef for the night. Two carronades were then taken out of her, and brought on board the corsair, and the captain was ordered to go to his ship, where the pirate wanted him.

55

I was compelled to accompany him in the boat, and, as we approached, one of the pirates on board threw a Dutch sailor into the sea. We picked up the poor wretch, and the Dutch captain put some question to him, at the reply to which they all gave a dismal groan, and exhibited the greatest terror and distress.

When we reached the ship, the captain was ordered on deck first, which he no sooner reached than he was knocked down and threatened with destruction if he did not reveal where the money was concealed, and the most dreadful threats made because he denied that there was any. I was then appealed to, and asked if I thought there was any; I answered in the negative. This seemed to pacify the pirate, who, however, said that he would detain the vessel, and discharge the cargo, consisting of gin, but-ter, cheese, and bales of canvas, and then burn her; and, with the most horrid imprecations, threatened the whole crew with death, if he found money after-wards.

The mate of the vessel had, during the pirate's stay on board, denied all knowledge of the English language, and had, no doubt, by that artifice escaped very many awkward questions. Of this circumstance, however, I was not aware & addressed some questions to him, which he unwittingly answered me. His replies were overheard by the captain, who, always alive to suspicions, now suspected that he had had some object in view in concealing his knowledge of our language. I endeavoured to protect the poor fellow, as I had been the cause of his detection, by saying, that he spoke so badly that I could scarcely understand him, and that, therefore, he had only spoken the truth. My interferences saved his life, but did not secure him from blows, of which he received his share. The suspicions of the pirate had, however, been roused, and nothing could persuade him but that the whole of the crew understood English more or less. In consequence of this unfortunate circumstance, the ship's cook underwent a great deal of rough usage and ill treatment, because he could not answer in English to some questions which were put to him, and which the captain, who was drunk, insisted should be answered in that language.

At dusk I was sent on board the corsair for the night, which passed without any remarkable occurrence. At four in the morning, the vessels weighed anchor, and went to the mouth of the channel, where they again brought to, and waited for the sea breeze, as they could not enter without a leading wind. At ten o'clock, the sea breeze blew rather fresh, and they entered the harbour, where the corsair was brought to an anchor, and the Dutch ship run on shore. A boat was then despatched for me, and on my arrival, the captain, who had passed the night on board, desired me to go below, and dress the wounds of one of the pirates whom he had punished for insolence during the night. When I went, I found the man had received a very severe cut with a sword on the side of the head, the wound extending from the left temple to the ear. When I had cleaned and dressed the wound, the fellow seemed very grateful for my attention, and said, that when he was well, he would assist me to escape; but I was too fearful of treachery to intimate a wish to that effect to him.

After dinner I was sent ashore to the magistrate; but, on our way thither, became an unwilling participater in an unexpected rencontre. As our boat was approaching the entrance of the narrow passage, which I have had occasion to mention before, we perceived another with six men rowing rapidly towards us from the shore.

Our first idea was that it was a man of war's boat, and the pirates made immediate preparation for defence, being apparently determined to sell their lives very dearly, consulting me upon what mode of fighting they should adopt, and insisting upon my being their leader. One of the men, however, recognized the chief mate as one of the party, and from their movements it appeared they were going to attack us. Knowing that indiscriminate slaughter would ensue, and that I should suffer the same as the rest, I consented to direct them how to defend their boat, & while considering on the best means of doing so, a musket was fired across our bows, and signals made for us to go to them. No time was to be lost; so I desired two of the men to lie down in the boat with their blunderbusses, and the other two to keep at the oars, having theirs ready by them to use at a pre-concerted signal; then taking the helm in my hand, guided the boat direct upon the others. When I found that the boat had sufficient way upon her, I desired the rowers to desist and take their weapons, and be ready to jump into the other, with their cutlasses, the instant that they had discharged their pieces. My instructions were fully obeyed, and the result was in our favour. The suddenness of our attack completely disconcerted them; three of them fell by our fire, the rest made but a feeble resistance, two of whom were instantly massacred by the pirates, & the other leaped into the sea, wounded as he was, and endeavoured to swim off, but was followed and taken. We only lost one man, who received a ball in the head, and instantly expired.

The unfortunate prisoner was interrogated as to the cause that had induced him to join the chief mate in his designs. He replied, that he had left the Havannah with no other view than to join the pirate; but having heard on shore of the unprovoked slaughter of their associates, they had determined to be revenged. When they observed the corsair bring in her prize, they knew that there would be frequent communications with the shore, and resolved to cut off the boats, seriatim, as fast as they were sent. He then declared that he had told them the truth, and hoped, that, as he was not the instigator of the deed, they would be satisfied with having taken the lives of his companions, and spare his own. But the appeal was made in vain, for he was almost instantaneously stabbed to the heart by one of the crew. Thus did I become the unwilling actor in a scene of blood, and assist, by my advice, in the destruction of six of my fellow creatures. I did then, & do now, often reflect upon it with horror; but I had no alternative, and must have been massacred myself had I not complied with the mandates of the ferocious wretches, among whom it was the misfortune of my life to be thrown. On our arrival on shore a hole was dug, and the murdered man buried. I was then placed upon a litter, as before, and taken to the magistrate's house. Seraphina and her mother met me at the door, and seemed rejoiced to see me, particularly the former. I found the old man in a very favourable state; and, having dressed his wounds, and informed his wife and daughter that there was no danger to be apprehended, retired to another room, where Seraphina joined me. To my inquiries, she told me that she had made preparations for our departure, and had engaged a guide, who had undertaken to conduct us for a hundred dollars; and that in eight or ten days we should be able to proceed. She was in raptures at the prospect of going to England; but not more so than myself.

The prize-master had been instructed to remain as short a time as possible on shore; and seeing that I had performed the service upon which I had been sent, informed me he was waiting for me. I begged a short delay, which he with much and evidently sincere regret denied his ability to grant; and I was consequently compelled to take an unwilling leave of my fair consoler. No accident befell us on our return; and as soon as we had arrived, the whole affair of our rencontre was detailed to the captain, who had been alarmed at the firing, and the success of it entirely attributed to the advice and skill of the Englishman. The captain appeared displeased when we first came on board; but this intelligence pleased him; and he told me that he had intended to punish me very severely for having told the Dutchman that he was a pirate; but on account of the services which I had rendered his boat's crew, he should forgive me and look it over; yet, if ever I did so again, nothing should save me. I now advanced more and more in the pirate's confidence, and hoped that this would at some time be favourable to my intended attempt to escape.

Two small coasting schooners, which the captain had seized for the purpose, were at this time receiving the prize's cargo on board, to convey to the Havannah for sale; and I was ordered to go and take account of it, as well as to superintend the unlading, and make the Dutch sailors work. By two o'clock in the morning, until which time they kept constantly at work, the lading of the schooners was completed, and I returned on board to sleep.

The following morning was a dead calm, and the sails of the Dutch ship were all unbent, and her topgallant-masts sent down over deck. About nine o'clock a breeze sprung up from the east, and soon after a large schooner hove in sight. I was ordered to the mast-head, as usual, to examine her, and reported her to be a large coasting schooner, very full of men. The whole of the Dutch vessel's crew were then ordered on board, with the exception of the captain, cook, the carpenter, who was lame, and a little boy. Several guns were brought up out of the hold, and the ship prepared for action. The Captain then went aloft himself, and soon discovered the schooner to be an old acquaintance, a fellow-pirate. He however suspected the peaceful disposition of the approaching corsair; and asked me, in case of attack, whether it would be prudent for him to remain at anchor. I answered in the negative; and the vessel was got under weigh, and the Dutchmen informed that they would be expected to take an active share in the engagement. They remonstrated, and some even cried at the mandate; but this only produced blows, and they were obliged to take their station at the guns. The schooner having hove to in a wide passage through which the stranger was to pass, awaited her arrival. As she drew near, we perceived a white flag at the mast-head as an amicable signal, which was answered by the red flag at the fore-top-mast-head, & a Spanish ensign at the peak, upon which the other hoisted out and despatched a boat with five men.

When about musket-shot from us, they paused as

if in doubt, and the helmsman waved a white flag, to which the captain replied with a white handkerchief, and beckoned him on board. The boats then came alongside, the two captains recognized each other, and the stranger smiled at our warlike preparations. Both vessels then stood into the harbour, and came to anchor, and were no sooner moored than the officers of the other came on board the corsair, and were well entertained. Before they proceeded to carouse, the captain informed me I must go on shore to the magistrate, and take with me such medicines as I thought he might require for the next four or five days, as he should convoy the two small schooners with the Dutchman's cargo on their way to the Havannah, and should not return for that time.

I willingly obeyed this order, and was conveyed in the usual manner on shore, and from thence to the village. After dressing the old man's wounds I had an interview, as usual, with Seraphina. I informed her of the probability of my being absent for some days, and begged her to expedite the preparations for our departure in the mean time. She was proceeding to assure me of her willingness to do every thing in her power, when a hasty messenger arrived, and brought orders for my instant return to the corsair, in consequence of an alarming accident on board. When I arrived, I found that the whole party had got extremely intoxicated; and the cry of a sail being made, the captain of the stranger had gone up into the rigging of his own ship to look out; and, having lost his hold, had fallen on deck, and was much bruised. He seemed dreadfully alarmed; but I pacified him, telling him that there was no danger; and, having bled him, put him to bed. He was very grateful for what I did, and offered to exert his interest for my release. As I knew the application would be fruitless, and might lead to ill treatment, I declined it. He then offered me money, which I also refused. The corsair now came to visit him, and the other begged I might be allowed to remain with him for this cruise, until he was recovered, pledging his word to bring me safe back; but the other refused, on the plea that he could not spare me.

After we had supped, the captain returned to his own vessel, taking me with him. Although, during the day, they had been upon the most friendly terms, and the stranger had received large presents of cheese, gin, butter, and even sails and spars, and almost every thing he might have deemed necessary; yet so suspicious was the pirate of the other having some sinister design upon him, that he took every precautionary measure in his power. Springs were put on his cable, the watch was doubled, the guns loaded, and the men ordered to lie with their arms upon the deck, which was cleared as if for immediate action. Whether it was, that the other had really had any hostile designs upon the corsair, and was prevented from putting them into execution by the activity and watchfulness of his rival, or that the suspicions of the captain were unjust or ill-founded, I do not know; but both parties remained tranquil for the night, although both appeared to be on their guard.

In the morning, I visited my new patient in the other vessel, who very gratefully offered to do all he could in his power for me. The captain arrived soon after, having been sent for by him, and I was very warmly recommended to his good graces. Both vessels in a short time began to prepare for their respective cruises; and the two pirates now took leave of one another, and the captain and myself returned on board our own schooner. After having left four of the crew as a guard in the prize, her own crew being on board the corsair, the pirate proceeded on his voyage to the Havannah, accompanied by the two small schooners. All three stood up within the reef till the afternoon, when we discovered a small schooner-rigged vessel, very full of men, coming down towards us. As she was too insignificant to cause any apprehension, the captain kept on his course until within gun-shot, and fired to bring her to. A boat was then despatched on board with ten of the Dutchmen armed; with orders to search for arms and ammunition; but on no account to injure the people on board of her. In boarding her, the Dutchmen drew their swords, which so alarmed some of the Spaniards that they jumped overboard; at which, the captain, who was watching them with a glass, laughed most heartily, pointing them out to me. He had the humanity, however, to despatch another boat to their assistance; and the prize-master, who went on this last service, informed us, when he returned, that he knew most of the people on board, who were inhabitants of some of the villages along the coast. At dusk, the convoy anchored for the night; and at day-break, again pursued their voyage.

We had proceeded but a very little way when we perceived a large schooner on the outer edge of the reef, & I was sent to my usual post on such occasions, to reconnoitre. She proved to be a merchantman; and as the wind was light, sweeps were got out, to go in chase of her. We were approaching her very fast, when we observed that she had despatched a small canoe with three men towards the shore. The captain no sooner perceived this than he manned and despatched a boat in pursuit; as he conjectured that they had specie on board. Having taken this measure, he hoisted the red flag, and fired a gun at the schooner, to bring her to. She immediately wore round, and hoisted Spanish colours, which made the pirate believe she would engage him; he cleared the vessel for action accordingly, and fired a second shot with intent to strike her, but it fell short, though well directed. The stranger now hauled down her colours and hove to, and the pirate hailed and ordered the captain on board with his papers.

On his arrival on board, they recognized one another as old friends; and when the pirate asked him what had induced him to despatch his canoe ashore, he found, by the reply, that his conjecture had been true. The stranger had taken him for a Carthagenian privateer; and had sent what little money he had on board, away. The boat in the mean time had gained upon the canoe, and having fired, wantonly too, a volley of musketry at her, had compelled the rowers to stop; but no mischief, fortunately, had ensued. After an interchange of civilities, the captain of the stranger returned, taking with him two cases of gin, and half a dozen cheeses as a present.

At night we anchored in a small bay, called by the Spaniards Morillia, about two leagues south-west of the Bay of Honde. As there were several piratical row-boats, that frequently capture small vessels, and infested the latter place, the pirate did not think his convoy out of danger until they had passed it, and therefore accompanied them thus far; and then, giving them in charge of the prize-master, returned towards the harbour, which we reached on the following evening. On his arrival there, he ran the corsair alongside the Dutch prize, and having taken out her guns and stores, had her hove down to repair some trifling damage done to her coppering; upon which the Dutch carpenter, and the one belonging to the pirate, were jointly employed.

On the following afternoon, while they were thus occupied, & the corsair was defenceless, an American sloop of war hove in sight, and stood close along the outer edge of the reef. I felt confident that she would send in her boats to attack the pirates, and trembled between hope & fear. Hope, because that event might procure me my liberty, and fear, lest being found among this horde of miscreants, my tale should be disbelieved, and myself confounded with them, and subjected to the same ignominious and disgraceful end. That she could not see the pirates and distinctly discern all their movements, I will never believe; for I could plainly perceive her men and officers walking the deck. Nay, so apprehensive were the pirates that they would be attacked, that they all gathered round & entreated the captain to right the schooner, and take measures of defence. The captain, however, appeared to know his man, and to hold him in thorough contempt. 'When I see them hoist out their boats,' cried he, 'I will believe they are in earnest; but the Americans always boast more than they perform, and they will not attempt to attack us; were they English, I should be afraid.' His conclusions were just; for the American took no notice whatever, and very quietly pursued his way.

With them ceased my hopes and my apprehensions; but Seraphina appeared to me in the shape of my delivering angel. In the course of the afternoon I went on shore to visit her father, whom I found much better; and having discharged my duty towards him, had my usual interview with my fair and amiable friend. Her eyes and her countenance beamed love and joy when she entered the room, and I immediately perceived that she had some welcome intelligence to communicate. 'I have arranged all,' cried she passionately, throwing herself into my arms, 'the guide is in readiness, and it only remains for us to fix the time and find the opportunity.' I clasped the dear lovely creature in my arms; I was too agitated to speak; and, while I held her to my heart, shed over her tears of joy and gratitude. She was the first who recovered her self-possession, &, blushing to find herself in that situation, gently disengaged herself from my arms, and advised me to be on my guard, and not let any one see my emotion. 'Do not be so agitated,' cried she, 'the time is short, and we have much to think of; therefore let us make the most of it to render our plans effective.' After many schemes had been proposed and rejected by turns, it was agreed that I should come over late on the second evening, under pretence of performing some surgical operation on her father; that she would in the mean time have the horses and guide in waiting at a short distance, and take every precaution to prevent a discovery. Our conversation was now interrupted by the entrance of several villagers, who, having heard of my cures, had come to me for medical advice. As I was cautious of giving umbrage to the captain, I declined giving any advice without his consent; and, to avoid importunity, told the prize-master, who always accompanied me as a guard, that I was ready to return on board the schooner.

On our arrival at the vessel we found a boat along-side, belonging to the magistrate of a village, about ten miles off; who had sent to beg some gin, cheese, and other articles, from the pirate. Anxious to keep on good terms at all times with these authorities, the boat was laden with presents and sent back. Can it be a matter of surprise that these miscreants have commit-ted their lawless depredations for so long a time, and with such impunity, when the very men whose duty it was to extirpate them, were daily encouraging them; when the pirate could boast that the magistrate was his friend, and receive, in the face of all the laws of his country and of nations, such proofs of his friendship, as to be enabled to thwart all hostile measures adopt-ed against him? European nations may send out their crusades against them; but while the execution of the laws is placed in such hands; while pirates plunder, and the magistrate and his myrmidons share; all their efforts will be vain; and, like the Hydra, when they destroy one head, a fresh one will supply its place.

The night passed without any particular occurrence, and in the morning the American sloop of war again hove in sight. The corsair's repairs had been completed the preceding day, and she had been righted; the captain, therefore, out of bravado, said, 'as the Yankee will not come to me, I will go to him.' I certainly expected that the experiment would cost him dear; but of his real object I was not aware until we had got without the reef. Having attracted the attention of the American, and induced him to chase the corsair, he ran into an intricate channel with the hopes of decoying him on the rocks. This he could do with impunity, as the pilots were well acquainted with every part of the reef. He made the experiment three or four times, but the American was too wary, and perceived his object. I thought, at least, that after this he would send in his boats; but, no; he took no further notice of him, and stood quietly on, although the pirate had actually fired at him, and insulted his flag. In the evening I finished the sail, which I had commenced some time before, at which I worked till bed time, and then stretched myself on my mattress, in anxious expectation of the day that was to restore me to liberty, & deliver me from the hands of these miscreants. The greatest part of the night was passed in sleepless agitation, between hope and fear, weighing in my mind every obstacle that might arise to oppose my escape, and the means to obviate them. Towards morning I sunk into a profound sleep, from which I did not wake till called to visit the sick. The wished-for and important moment was now fast approaching, and I told the pirate that I should want to go on shore, to perform some necessary operations upon the magistrate. After some trifling questions, leave was granted; and, at five in the evening, with a beating heart, I descended the corsair's side, as I hoped for the last time.

On our arrival at the house, I found my reception unusually cold and formal; the mother looked at me with an air of anger and distrust, and Seraphina stood behind her, pale, and her cheeks bathed in tears. The moment she caught my eye, she made a signal to me to be silent, and in the most anxious agitation I passed into the sick man's chamber. 'Well, sir,' said he, 'I have detected you in your base and nefarious plans.' My presence of mind did not forsake me; I pretended not to understand him, &, with an assumed appearance of alarm and surprise, exclaimed, 'Good God, sir, I hope you are not delirious; I hope your wound has not taken an unfavourable turn'; and, taking him by the pulse, immediately pulled out a lancet, saying I must bleed him, as he was in a high fever.

The coolness and presence of mind with which I uttered this, completely staggered him, & he actually seemed to believe himself to be delirious, and that all was the effect of a disordered mind. He then asked me if I had made such proposals to his daughter. 'Sir,' I replied, with my former coolness, 'your suspicions are an insult to your daughter; for, had I been bold and villainous enough to have made such a proposal, she would have rejected it with contempt, and been the first to have informed you of it.' Seraphina, who had been listening, now entered the room, and he addressed himself to her; and she boldly, and with an indignant air, denied the accusation. 'What,' exclaimed the astonished father, 'did not the very guide you hired inform me?' 'Sir,' replied she, bursting into tears, 'that guide, as you call him, is a base and infamous wretch, and I will no longer screen him from your displeasure; he met me in the forest the other day, and took some very indecent liberties with me; and because I threatened to make it known to you, declared he would tell you that I wanted to elope with the Englishman. That I highly esteem him, I do not deny; & it would be ungrateful if I did not, after he has saved your life.' Here she sobbed loudly, & the old magistrate so completely believed her, that the mother was called in, and all matters amicably settled, the old man vowing vengeance against the rascally guide. The report of my intended escape had, however, transpired; and, as my not performing any operation on the magistrate might give a colour to it, I thought proper to bleed him, telling him that his blood was in a bad state, & required it. Seraphina took an opportunity of informing me that the guide she had engaged had insisted upon having fifty dollars in advance; and, having paid it him, he had no sooner received the money, than he basely betrayed her secret. She told me, however, that she would endeavour to obtain a more faithful one, and, in the mean time, begged I would place the utmost reliance on her exertions, and on her discretion. She had now given such proofs of her sincerity as well as of her firmness, that I did not doubt her; and although I left her disappointed, still I was not hopeless.

I saw that my attendants were grown excessively suspicious of me, and watched my motions closely; but I took no notice of it, and proceeded as usual to the boat. One thing, however, threw a gloom over my mind; the captain had declared, that when my services were no longer wanted, he would kill me, as it would be dangerous to let me escape, now I had obtained a knowledge of the reefs; for I should lead the English

71

men of war there. This proposal had been rejected by the prize-master and some of the crew, whose good will I had gained. This intelligence I had received in confidence from the cook; and I now dreaded that this report would afford a pretext for my murder. The captain's behaviour, however, was different from what I expected. At first, he was violent; but, on my repeating Seraphina's statement to the magistrate, and the prize-master confirming mine of having bled the old man, he became pacified, but declared that the magistrate must come to me for the future; he then ordered me to go below to bed.

On the following day, the crew were chiefly employed in lading boats sent by the priests & magistrates of the different villages, with gin, cheeses, and other presents, and nothing of consequence occurred.

On the day after, the other prize-master returned from the Havannah, with a merchant schooner, the owner of which was come to purchase the remainder of the Dutchman's cargo. The assassin who had been despatched to murder Mr. Lumsden, returned on board of her, and reported that his intended victim had sailed some time before his arrival. The schooner was loaded in the course of that day; and, on my making up the account of the purchase, the captain desired me to tell the crew that the amount was eight hundred dollars less than it really was, with a threat to murder me, if I betrayed the secret.

On the following morning, the schooner having completed her cargo, sailed for the Havannah, and was convoyed by the pirate as far as the Morillia, when he left her to proceed by herself, and anchored in the Bay. On that afternoon, the third mate of the corsair left the vessel, to proceed over land on a party of pleasure, and was to stop, for that evening, at a small village called Cavancas. I have reason to believe, however, that it was something more than a mere party of pleasure that had taken him to the Havannah.

The succeeding day presented another scene of atrocity and murder. In the morning, while at anchor, a sail was discovered in the offing; and, in order to alter the sailing of the schooner, the crew were employed in removing some of the ballast more aft. In this place the French cook of the Dutch prize was placed for security; as, since his capture, the ill treatment which he had undergone, and terror combined, had affected his mind, and he had shown evident symptoms of insanity. The inhuman wretches teazed the poor maniac until they made him rave, & in his frenzy he caught hold of a hatchet and wounded one of his tormentors. The blow was no sooner given than the rest plunged their knives into his body, and threw him overboard while yet breathing, accompanying their barbarity with most horrid expressions. I was on the top during this scene, but was called down to dress the wounded man.

Having performed this task, I returned to my station; but the morning was hazy, & it was long before I could obtain a distinct view of the stranger. The captain, however, had been up, and ascertained her to be an English brig, with full quarters, and a white streak. The vessel was then got under weigh, and the deck cleared for action. While this was doing, the gunner informed him that there were not cartridges enough made up for a long action, should she resist; and the novel task was assigned me to assist in making more. While thus employed, another vessel was seen, and I was called up to look at her; she also proved to be an English brig. The vessel of which we were in chase, however, still continued her course, and took no notice of the corsair, although several guns had been fired, and American colours hoisted. The captain was furious, & ordered another gun to be fired, of which she took no notice. The wind was light, and sweeps were then ordered out to gain upon her. As we approached, the long gun was shotted and fired, which produced the desired effect, and the brig brought to. The American colours were then hauled down, and the red flag hoisted, and the boat let down to board her. Six armed men were ordered into her for that purpose, and myself and a pilot directed to accompany them. I wished to avoid this unpleasant duty, but, on appearing to hesitate, was threatened with a repetition of the cruelties I had already undergone. With a bursting heart I complied, & was enjoined, with the most dreadful threats, to hold no communication with the captain or crew, while the pilot was directed to throw the former overboard; and, when he had tacked the brig towards shore to send me back. On our way, I prevailed upon the pilot, with whom I had some influence, to disobey the dreadful mandate. When we reached her, we were met by the captain of the brig at the gangway, who asked us who and what we were; to which I was obliged to give an evasive answer, by saying, that the corsair was a privateer.

After we had been on board the brig a short time, and had tacked her towards the shore, a musket was fired from the corsair, and I was desired by the pilot to tell the captain and his crew to go into the boat, and go on board the pirate. The captain, who had been regarding me stedfastly for some time, now claimed acquaintance with me. His face appeared familiar to me, I must confess, but his name I did not know; and, being well aware that all my motions were watched, I deemed it most prudent, for the present, to plead ignorance. Fearful that the pirate's boat would be too crowded, I recommended the captain to lower his own boat; but he declined, saying it was leaky, and not in a condition to go on the water. We then left the brig, the captain expressing a wish that he should not be long detained, and still apparently ignorant of the schooner being a pirate; to which I replied, I could not answer, as the captain was angry with him for having given so much trouble. On our reaching the corsair's deck, the pirate, in a rough tone, asked him his name, and he replied, Cooke; I then recognized him as a casual acquaintance. From the fury in which I saw the pirate, I anticipated the most serious consequences to the poor fellow; and, in order to save him, if possible, claimed relationship, and told him he was my cousin, and that, therefore, for my sake, and in consideration of the services that I had done for him, he would not maltreat Captain Cooke. For once I prevailed over his brutal disposition, & he promised not to do so, if the other told him the whole truth as to what money he had, and what was his cargo. The bills of lading were then handed to me, and I informed him that it consisted of rum only.

Having been informed by Captain Cooke that the vessel in sight was either a transport with troops, or the brig *Vittoria* from Black River, Jamaica, I was sent up to examine, and from her appearance pronounced her to be the transport. Captain Cooke was, however, ordered to look at her, and he, being better acquainted with the vessel, said it was the *Vittoria*, and chase was given immediately; much, however, against the will of the crew, who were afraid of her being the transport. The crew of the *Industry*, the vessel he had just captured, were ordered to the guns, in case of an engagement; and the corsair, for the breeze had now freshened, fast approached her chase. Notwithstanding the promise he had made, the pirate still exhibited an inclination to vent his fury on Captain Cooke, and I was occasionally obliged to interfere to save him from its effects.

I have been told, since my arrival in this country, that Captain Cooke has declared and boasted that he resisted the pirate, and did not quit his vessel, until a round shot had been fired between his masts, and a volley of musquetry on his deck. I am willing to give him every credit for his anxiety to save his vessel, and am ready to acknowledge that he did all that an unfortunate man in his situation could do; but I must deny the truth of his assertions on this point. The shot that was fired, was across the bow of the *Industry*, and fell short by more than a hundred yards; and, as to musquetry, with the solitary exception of the signal to the captain and crew on board, none was discharged. As for resistance, none whatever was made, and for a good reason – it was out of his power to make any.

The corsair, being a very rapid sailer, soon came within range of the *Vittoria*, and the long gun was fired athwart her bows, which she answered by hoisting her colours and breaking her mainyard. A pilot, for we had several, was then ordered to repair on board, accompanied by me, with directions to send the brig's officers, and part of her crew, on board. Our arrival was a signal for a repetition of the same brutal act towards the unfortunate crew of this vessel, that had been exercised towards those of the other; and the officers and some of the men were driven into the boat. The sails were then filled and the brig steered after the corsair, who was now returning towards the coast in the direction of Cape Blanco.

Soon after this, the atmosphere became dense and hazy, and it began to rain; and we were suddenly thrown into great alarm by the appearance of a strange schooner, who seemed to chase us. The man who was at first at the wheel had been changed, and his successor was not so good a steersman. As the wind was abaft the beam, we set steering sails by the pilot's direction, to get away from the stranger: but the man steered so badly, that the pirate began to be apprehensive of capture, and rated him for his awkwardness. The furious gesticulations of the Spaniard only confused the poor fellow, and made him steer worse. This added fuel to fire, and he began to suspect it was I that was making him do so, to enable the schooner to overtake us. He then turned upon me, and told me that if I did not make him steer more steadily, he would take his knife and kill him. I knew that to threaten, with these wretches, was to perform; in order, therefore, to save the man's life, I pretended to be enraged with him, and struck him lightly across the back with the flat part of a cutlass. This act, though done with the best and purest of motives, and from a desire to save the life of a fellow creature, has since been adduced against me, as a proof that I joined in the brutalities of these blood-stained miscreants, and took a delight in them. Such is the gratitude that man has to expect from his fellow man.

It was now late in the day; the rain had ceased, and

the atmosphere had become more clear, and with it our apprehensions had vanished; for we could perceive that the stranger was no man of war, nor was she in pursuit of us, but standing a different course. I began to wish that night would come on, for I had resolved in my own mind to attempt my escape under cover of the darkness; to kill the pilot and the other Spaniard, for only two were on board, & take the vessel to New Orleans. This I hoped to accomplish, as I counted upon the assistance of the two men who had been left on board. The pirate, however, was too guarded; for, at dusk, the gunner of the corsair was sent on board, and I was taken back. The prisoners on board were ordered down into the hold, with the exception of the steward of the *Industry*, who was sent into the cabin. Sentries were then placed over the hatchways, and the prisoners charged, on the peril of their lives, not to come upon deck.

All three vessels came to anchor close by each other, outside the reef; & as soon as the necessary arrangements were made for their safety, a council was held to deliberate on the disposal of the prisoners. Some question having arisen, I was sent for to inform them what quantity of coffee was in the *Vittoria*, and how much rum on board the *Industry*, with the relative value of each. On being informed, the captain declared the rum not worth their attention, and talked of destroying the latter vessel. I remained to hear the result of their deliberations, anxious for the safety of the unfortunate wretches who, like myself, had fallen into their hands. The debate was warm; part wished to put them to death and throw them overboard, and part, more merciful, wished that the *Industry* might be suffered to proceed, and take them with her. I joined

my entreaties to this effect; and, after much altercation, the latter alternative was chosen, much to the
dissatisfaction of the more sanguinary party. The
sentinels prevented any communication with the
English prisoners, so that I could not inform them of
their fate. I was then ordered below, and the captain
left the corsair to visit the two brigs, leaving her in
charge of the prize-master.

On his return he told me that he should grant my
request, and give up the *Industry*; and then gave
orders to the prize-master to that effect, giving strict
injunctions, however, to detain the clothes of both the
crews. He then went on shore, as he said, to overtake
the third mate at the Cavannias, and to give him
instructions to send vessels down from the
Havannah, with bags, for the purpose of sending the
Vittoria's coffee to market.

I dreaded much that the captain's absence would
be the cause of the ill treatment, if not of the murder
of the prisoners on board; nor were my fears without
foundation. One of the fiends who had wished to put
them to death, now proposed to carry the diabolical
plan into immediate execution, but was opposed by
the prize-master in charge. Deeming him the only
obstacle, he watched his opportunity, and while he was
reclining against one of the guns, made an attempt to
despatch him with his knife. The blow, fortunately for
us all, failed, and the cries of his intended victim
roused the crew to his assistance, who inflicted summary justice on the blood-thirsty miscreant, and in
their fury put him instantly to death.

This attempt so alarmed me, that I kept awake
the remainder of the night, as also did the *Industry*'s
steward, who was in the cabin with me. We drew as

close together as we dared, and conversed in low whis-
pers during the night, ceasing, however, when we
heard anyone approach; and I took that opportunity of
communicating my unfortunate situation, and what I
had suffered since I had been a prisoner; with which
he seemed much affected, and sincerely pitied my
case. In the morning, the crew of both vessels, with
the exception of Captain Hearn, his mate, a passenger,
& the *Industry*'s steward, were employed in getting
the *Vittoria* under weigh. Seeing Captain Hearn upon
deck, I obtained leave of the prize-master to address
him. I then informed him of my unfortunate situation;
and told him that I should escape the first favourable
opportunity. At his request, I obtained his coffee certificates for him from the prize-master; but could not
succeed in obtaining the restoration of any part of
their clothes, which the pirates were resolved to keep.
Between one and the other, I was often placed in an
awkward dilemma; if I applied for the restoration of
any part of the plunder, the pirates became exasperated, and I incurred the risk of ill treatment: if; on the
other hand, for the sake of my personal safety, I
declined any interference, I was immediately charged
with a want of feeling, and the motives misrepres-
ented. That such has been the case, I have had good
reason to know; and the prejudices which these
misrepresentations excited, were nearly fatal to me on
a recent occasion.

The corsair and the *Vittoria* were now under
weigh, and the prisoners, except the Dutchmen,
having performed the task assigned to them, had
been transferred on board the *Industry*; the prize-
master therefore desired me to hail Captain Cooke, and
to tell him that he was at liberty to pursue his voyage.

Although it was in a great measure owing to my interference, and that too at the risk of my own life and personal safety, that the lives of himself and the rest had been spared, and his vessel given back to him; yet, since my return to this country, when I was standing on peril of my life, this man did not show the common feelings of gratitude. I received even more kindness from the pirates themselves, brutes as they were, than from this man. Not content with misrepresentations & misstatements, wilful and premeditated, he has even had the audacity to invent most atrocious falsehoods, in order to poison the minds of those whose duty it was to sit in judgment upon me.

The corsair & her prize stood along the reef towards Rio O'Media; but as the former was the fastest sailer, she soon shot ahead, and the other was left to come up after her. In the afternoon, another English vessel hove in sight; but as she was too far in the offing to come up with her before dark, the pirates would not go in chase, but continued on their course to the harbour; where she arrived in the evening, and let go her anchor near their former prize. As the *Vittoria* was not expected till the morning, in consequence of her heavy sailing, no anxiety was felt on her account, during the night; but her non-appearance in the morning excited surprise, as well as fear; and conjecture was busy deciding on her fate. A messenger, in the mean time, arrived from the magistrate for me; but the prize-master replied that the captain had forbidden my going on shore.

About two o'clock in the afternoon, the corsair's boat, containing the men that had been left in charge of the *Vittoria*, was seen coming towards us; and it was then imagined that she had been re-captured, and that they had therefore abandoned her. On enquiry, however, it appeared that they had taken the vessel we had seen the day before, for a ship of war, and, fearful of the consequences, had run the *Vittoria* on the reef; and, having abandoned her, left the Dutchmen on board to be retaken. This act of cowardice highly exasperated the pirates on board, who rated them severely, and would have returned in the corsair to the spot, had not the captain been hourly expected.

During the confusion excited by this event, the old magistrate arrived, & was received with due honours by the prize-master. He descended into the cabin to have his wound dressed; and, while I was so employed, informed me that he had taken measures to have the man punished who had circulated the scandalous report about his daughter and myself. After apologizing for his conduct on that occasion, he informed me that he should pay me a visit shortly, accompanied by Seraphina. He then returned on shore, taking with him presents of gin and cheeses.

About midnight, the pirates were thrown into an alarm by the arrival of a boat, which proved to be the Dutchmen, who had been driven out of the *Vittoria* by fishermen, who came to plunder her. A boat with eight armed men was immediately despatched to protect the prize; but she had already been plundered of eight tierces of coffee.

I have been informed that Captain Hearn and his crew were put on board a man of war by the *Industry*, a few days after her release. If so, why was not search made after the pirates and their prizes, and the latter recaptured. For seven days, she remained not five leagues from the place where she was captured; and, what is still more important, on the exterior edge of the reef; & exposed to view. Perhaps it was anticipated that the pirates had plundered her of her cargo; and that therefore the salvage would not have been sufficient to repay them for their trouble. Is not this a very strong proof of the gross and culpable negligence of the admiral and officers upon that station. Ships of war, forsooth, could be found at all times, and ready at a very short notice, to convey specie, and when so employed, would make direct voyage, and pay no attention to that duty upon which they had been sent—the protection of mercantile property. Well might the merchants and the underwriters complain; but of what avail were those complaints, when such open and glaring dereliction of duty was daily and hourly committed, and glossed over by the Lords of the Admiralty, instead of being inquired into & severely punished? Private interest was, however, considered of more importance; and the public commerce, the trade of the country, appeared as nothing when put in competition with it. How many lives have been sacrificed, how many thousand pounds worth of property plundered, and how much misery and suffering to individuals has this daring breach of a public duty occasioned! But to my narrative.

The captain not having returned on the following morning, the schooner weighed and ran down to the *Vittoria*: and on the same day two vessels arrived for the coffee from the Havannah. These were immediately laden, and the *Vittoria* having become lighter in consequence of the discharge of so much of her cargo, floated off the reef. Sail was immediately made on her, and both vessels directed their course towards Rio O'Media the next day. In the afternoon, however, the Jamaica fleet hove in sight, and the *Vittoria* was once more drawn on the outer edge of the reef; while the corsair stood in and anchored. Here again was another culpable instance of neglect: the whole fleet, with the man of war at their head, passed within a league of the place, where the *Vittoria* was lying full in their view, & evidently a prize to the pirates; yet no notice whatever was taken. At that moment one boat would have captured both vessels, as a great number of the corsair's crew were absent, and his means of defence were consequently weakened.

The piracies in the Rio O'Media had now become too notorious for the government to countenance them any longer; and a body of police was consequently despatched, bringing with them instructions to the magistrates to give them every assistance in their search for plundered property. This information no sooner reached the old magistrate, than he sent down to the Dutch vessel, took out the men on board, and despatched them to the corsair, & then set fire to her where she was. She soon burned to the water's edge, and then floating, was carried away by the current, so that not a vestige remained. The *Vittoria*, in the mean time, had been got off the reef a second time, and, having been brought into the harbour, was run upon a mud bank; while the corsair gave notice to the inhabitants of her safe return, by discharging her guns. A message soon after arrived from the captain at Casso Blanco, desiring that the Dutchman might be instantly set at liberty, & sent away on board a small vessel belonging to the pirates, and that a boat might be despatched for him. This messenger informed us that a party of police, thirty in number, had been searching through the villages for plundered property; but as soon as the report of the corsair's guns had reached their ears, they made a precipitate retreat. Such was the dependence that was to be placed on those cowardly wretches.

The Dutch prisoners were released, and sent away the following day; but what became of them I never heard. Whether they succeeded in reaching their native shore; or whether they were, like myself, apprehended on charges of piracy, as they had assisted as well in several captures, and were not so fortunate in being able to establish their innocence, is a question that I am unable to answer. They were released, however, according to the order, and I envied them their fate.

The magistrate and Seraphina soon after visited us; the former confirmed the tale of the messenger relative to the conduct of the police. They were accompanied by a number of young ladies, who, Seraphina informed me, having heard of my case, had come to consult me. She lamented bitterly our disappointment, and told me that the cause of it was now suffering for his perfidy, in a prison.

Two priests and a magistrate, accompanied by four females, added to the number of the company on board. These visits appeared to be for the sake of getting what they could from the pirates. The priests, as usual, exercised all the chicanery of their craft, and were well paid for it. They visited the *Vittoria*, and took all her charts and maps for household ornaments, and having returned on board, caroused till dusk, when the whole party took their leave.

On the second day, the captain returned, and was

furious, when informed of the circumstances of the *Vittoria*; so much so, that the pilot who had been on board of her narrowly escaped with his life. The third mate soon after arrived with two coasting vessels from the Havannah, which were speedily loaded with the remainder of the *Vittoria*'s cargo. The pirates, at all times, found great facility in disposing of their plunder, by these coasting vessels, who were always ready not only to receive it, but also frequently lent their crews to assist in the capture and to board vessels.

A whole week had nearly passed without any remarkable occurrence, when another piratical schooner entered Rio O'Media. Her captain informed us that he had plundered three English vessels, out of one of which he had detained a carpenter, who, he said, was an excellent workman. This unfortunate wretch I did not see; but I was informed that he was assassinated as soon as he had completed the task for which he had been detained, and I have no reason to disbelieve it.

From the conversation of the pirate, I learned the system on which these vessels are fitted out. He informed our captain that he had entered into an agreement with the owner to put guns, muskets, and every other article, secretly on board at the Havannah, and then clear her out, as it were for a neighbouring port, in charge of a master. At night, when she anchored along the coast, he boarded and took possession of her, setting the master ashore. The owner, on receiving the intelligence, made a complaint to the governor that his vessel was seized by pirates; & the master confirming it by his statement every body believed it to be the fact; while the other was sharing the plunder, without the suspicion of being *particeps criminis*. Having completed her fitting out with sails and spars from the *Vittoria*, at the end of five days the pirate took his departure.

A few days after, the corsair captured a French vessel, from Vera Cruz, with a large quantity of specie on board. The Frenchman was rather obstinate in his endeavour to conceal the money, and I witnessed a repetition of the brutality practised on former occasions, by which means a confession was extorted, and the specie found. The money on board was chiefly in dollars, and the captain sent word on shore that he would give a premium of four dollars on every doubloon. This favourable rate of exchange soon brought priests & magistrates on board, particularly the former; and these holy men, by these means, became partakers of one-fourth of the plunder.

I became at this time very ill with an attack of fever, and my wounds broke out afresh. I attributed this to the closeness of the ship, from the prisoners being kept constantly below; and, for the sake of my own health, as well as others, suggested it to the captain, who allowed them to walk the deck during the day. When I had recovered a little, an American brig fell into their hands; but the captain having at once delivered up his money, and pointed out the most valuable part of his cargo, was very well treated by the pirate. His watch, however, had attracted the notice of the prize-master; and, as he did not surrender that so readily, he was on the point of being assassinated; but, to save his life, he gave it up, although he wanted to recover it, when released subsequently, declaring, on that occasion, that he had only lent it under promise of having it restored, when done with. The crew of the French vessel was transferred to the American on the following day, and she was piloted out of the reef, and allowed to go on her voyage.

An attack of intermittent fever shortly after confined me to my mattress. Under this fit of illness I laboured for fifteen days, and was much reduced. During all this time I was left to shift for myself, but experienced much kindness and attention from Seraphina, who, when she heard of my illness, frequently visited me, and brought with her every little thing that she thought might conduce to my comfort. When I had partially recovered, I solicited permission to go on shore; but the request was brutally denied, under the plea that I only wished to escape.

Soon after this refusal, while I was on deck one very calm morning, a schooner was discovered in the offing. I was peremptorily ordered aloft to look at her, and had begun to ascend the rigging: but so weak and exhausted was I, that I expected to fall every moment. The captain observed my condition, and for once had the humanity to desire me to remain on deck, and went aloft himself. When he came down, a boat with armed men was despatched to board, as it was a dead calm, and the corsair would have made very little way herself had her anchor been weighed. The boat's crew took possession of her without any resistance, although the schooner was large, and well manned. A breeze springing up soon after they were in possession, they brought their prize into the harbour, when the captain went on board of her.

As soon as he returned, he informed me that the prize was an American, and that she had on board of her, as passengers, a Spanish officer and his wife; but the latter, he added, was extremely ill, from sea sickness and the bad treatment of the captain, who had been brute enough to deny her many little comforts, and requested I would go on board and prescribe for her. He was much exasperated against the captain for this act, and was determined to murder him; and the finding no money on board tended not a little to confirm him in his resolution.

In a short time, however, the officer and his wife were brought on board the corsair, and I was saved the fatigue of visiting the prize. I confess I had no difficulty in prescribing for her, nourishment being all that she required; but she was evidently in a delicate state of health. Her husband appeared to be a great brute, and to care very little about her, as he began to drink & carouse with the pirates almost as soon as he came on board, paying no attention to his wife. I took the opportunity of my attending on her to inform her of the captain's threat, and prevailed upon her to join her entreaties with mine that the American's life might be spared. She did so when the pirate visited her; and at our joint solicitation he escaped that summary punishment which he had drawn down upon his head for his unfeeling conduct to this poor woman.

It was customary with the pirate to make the crew of a prize, if possible, drunk, in order, in that unguarded moment, to obtain from them a knowledge of all that was on board. He had on this occasion been very liberal in his allowance of spirits to the crew of the schooner, who were prisoners on board, and were partly Irish. Intoxication soon led to quarrelling, and a fight then took place, which afforded very great merriment to the pirates who laughed very heartily at it. The officer and his wife had a mattress prepared for them next to mine in the cabin, where they slept that night. To the latter I was very assiduous in my attentions, and made up little messes of arrow root and wine, and did all in my power to administer to her comfort. For these attentions she was remarkably grateful, but manifested a degree of warmth in her gratitude that I was fearful would lead to serious consequences.

One night, after we had retired to our respective mattresses, I was surprised, when I awoke about midnight, to find the lady by my side, and her arm thrown round my neck, fast asleep. I awakened her gently, and respectfully informed her of her mistake. She made no reply, but returned to the side of her lawful spouse. I looked upon this as a mere accident arising from the contiguity of our mattresses, and therefore thought no more of it. On the following night, however, I was again roused from my slumbers by her caresses; but on this occasion the consequences were nearly fatal to me. The husband awoke just at the same instant, and missing his wife, and seeing her by my side, vociferated so loudly as to awaken both her and the captain; but I thought it most prudent for myself to counterfeit sleep. At her first awakening, she gave a faint scream; but soon recovered her presence of mind, and succeeded in pacifying her enraged husband, whom she convinced that the mistake had occurred in her sleep, and that his honor remained uninjured, which he the more readily believed, from my being apparently asleep. The pirate, who at first had felt inclined to treat the matter seriously, now burst into a loud laugh, in which I could scarce refrain from joining. For several days the corsair remained out at sea, having on board the American crew, and cruised backwards and forwards, in hope of falling in with the

Peacock, of New York, which the captain of the prize had informed the pirate was to touch at the Havannah, and was richly laden, having besides a large quantity of specie on board. Whether the other had invented the information with the hope of being more speedily liberated, or whether the *Peacock* had been fortunate enough to escape the pirate's vigilance, I do not know; but, after an ineffectual cruise of some days, he returned into harbour, and gave up the pursuit. In revenge, he plundered the schooner he had captured; and having taken out every thing of any value, he gave her up to the crew, & ordered them to go to New Orleans; but on the peril of their lives not to pursue their voyage to the Havannah. The Spanish officer, when he heard the mandate, begged to be detained on board, & to be sent thither the first favourable opportunity. As the pirate did not apprehend any bad consequences from this indulgence, his request was granted, and the American sailed without him.

Ever since the occurrences of that evening, the

Spaniard kept a jealous eye upon his fair partner; and I was equally reserved and cautious in my communications with her. But her own imprudence had nearly rendered all my precautions abortive. I was below in the cabin, mixing some medicine for a sick man, when the lady slipped from her husband and came down. She had no sooner entered the cabin, than she seated herself on my knee, and very familiarly putting her arm round my neck, gave me a kiss. The officer, who had followed her almost the instant she left him, entered at the moment, & with most furious gesticulation rushed upon deck, and called upon the captain to inflict summary punishment upon me. The lady, however, stood my friend on this occasion as on the former, and declared that her husband must have been mistaken, as no such thing had occurred. She then explained the cause of being seen on my knee, and said that she had slipped in consequence of the motion of the vessel, and I had caught her in my arms, & had saved her from falling and seriously hurting herself. As there was a swell, and the vessel occasionally gave a lurch, the tale had the air of probability, and the captain declared that punishment was out of the case. The officer put on a constrained air of satisfaction; but I was convinced he would watch an opportunity of revenge, and was not at all sorry when, on the following day, he took his departure in a coasting schooner, his expences being defrayed by the pirate.

All this time the *Vittoria* lay on the mud bank, exposed to the full view of every ship that passed; yet no attempts were made to re-capture her. The pirate used often to say in joke that the naval officers on the station thought it better amusement to drink and enter into every species of debauchery at the Havannah, than to look after pirates, or attempt to attack them; and, from what I myself experienced, I verily believe the assertion to be fact.

Nothing of importance occurred for several days, & the corsair remained quietly at anchor. One night, however, a letter was brought from the magistrate, intimating that the governor of the Havannah had adopted hostile measures, and that one hundred soldiers were expected over land, and that five gun boats were to come down inside the reef, in four or five days; and therefore advised him to be on his guard. On the following morning, the magistrate himself came on board, and added, that he had received the most positive orders to render every assistance, by information or otherwise, to this armament. He then advised the captain to destroy the *Vittoria* as soon as ever the forces approached, of which he would give him a signal.

The pirate now became apprehensive for his own safety, and resolved to go to Cape Saint Antonio for a while. This resolution he communicated to the magistrate, & obtained a promise from him to send a boat with communications of all that might occur in his absence. These preliminaries having been arranged, preparations were made for sailing, and the magistrate took his leave. On the following morning, we proceeded outside the reef down to Cape St. Antonio, and came to an anchor off that place. The magistrate, who was apprehensive of consequences, destroyed the *Vittoria* the day after the pirate sailed. The corsair had lain at anchor for ten days; but still no information reached her of the expected armament, and all began to look upon it as a false alarm. About nine o'clock of the evening of the eleventh day, however, the promised boat arrived, to inform the pirate that he might expect the gun boats at Cape St. Antonio on the following day. After having performed his mission, the messenger immediately returned, in order to pass the boats unobserved while it was dark; and every preparation was made on board to prevent surprise.

The morning was fine, clear, and calm. There was not a ripple on the sea; its surface was like a mirror, and not a breath of air was stirring. The gun boats were discovered at an early hour, pulling towards the corsair, who did not seem disposed to await their arrival. The anchor was quickly weighed, and with her sweeps she was taken without the reef. The boats were about three miles from her, and, with a glass, all the movements could be distinctly observed. Had the officers who commanded them possessed the least spirit of enterprise, the corsair must have fallen into their hands; but my firm belief is that they were as much afraid of attacking the pirate, as he was that they would attack him. He had become desperate, & had resolved upon not yielding easily declaring he would do his utmost to sink them. At noon, a breeze sprung up, of which the corsair took advantage, and ran for Rio O'Media, while the gun boats came to an anchor.

The anchor was scarcely down, when the magistrate was on board to inform the captain that the *Vittoria*'s capture was unknown to the troops and gun boats, as she was totally destroyed before their arrival, and that the latter would remain off the Cape for some days. Having so far obliged his friend, he departed, promising to repeat his visit on the following day, accompanied by several others; who were coming to congratulate him.

The night was spent in watchfulness, and the day brought the promised party, consisting of the old magistrate & his daughter, with three or four ladies, and several other magistrates and priests. The whole were well entertained on board, and the latter were by no means sparing of the wines and spirits that were set before them. Seraphina seized the first opportunity of informing me of all that she had done during my absence, and raised my hopes by saying that she had engaged another & more trust-worthy guide for our escape, & that it only wanted an opportunity to avail ourselves of his services. We dwelt upon this interesting theme, devising the means, when a general movement for departure broke off our conversation. She took a warm and affectionate leave of me for the night, and this was the last interview I had with this kind, warm-hearted, and benevolent creature. Her kindness soothed me in my captivity, and I shall never forget her.

On the following morning, the corsair sailed for the Morillia, where she remained idle for nearly three weeks. At the end of that time, a French vessel fell into the hands of the pirate. The usual scene of cruelty and atrocity took place; and, when they had taken all the money, and the valuable part of her cargo, and destroyed and damaged the remainder, they cut away her mizen mast, and starboard main rigging, and in that crippled state dismissed them to pursue their voyage, forbidding them, however, to go to the Havannah.

The pirate returned with his plunder into the Morillia, where he anchored. Discord, however, began to rear her head among this horde of savages. Some one had insinuated that they had not been fairly dealt

by, & that the captain had secreted large sums for
himself. Discontent manifested itself, first, in whis-
pered insinuations, and, at last, in open accusations;
and two parties were consequently formed, one who
believed him innocent, and the other guilty. Things
were in this state, and each waiting only for a plau-
sible pretext to attack the other, when murder and
massacre would have ensued; but an unexpected
event suspended the quarrel. The man at the mast
head descried the gun boats steering towards the
corsair, and they were shortly after heard to scale
their guns. These warlike preparations seemed to
denote an immediate attack, and their private ani-
mosities were forgotten in the hurry of self-defence.
The alarm, however, was without foundation; for they
all passed on without noticing the pirate. A fisherman,
who boarded the schooner soon after, informed us that
the commanding officer of the flotilla had told him
that he was well aware that the schooner was a pirate,
but that he had no time to go in chase of her, as he was
on his return. Thus ended this boasted expedition for
the suppression of piracy, without effecting one single
object for which it was furnished and sent out. And no
wonder; for I am convinced, from personal observation, that, from the governor to the mere clerk or
officer, all derive some degree of benefit from the
acts of those lawless ruffians; and therefore it is
against their interest to injure them.

The discontent that existed previous to the late
alarm, now broke out afresh, and the two parties
would have proceeded to extremities, but for the
timely arrival of two gentlemen from the Havannah,
who I understood were the owners of the corsair. By
their interference, all differences were arranged; and

the newly acquired plunder being shipped on board two coasting vessels, they returned with them.

The captain, on the following day, was attacked by a fever, and felt himself so indisposed that he was apprehensive of death. He sent for me in a terrible state of alarm, and promised me my liberty if I cured him. The promise I knew would be broken the moment he was well, so I resolved to take advantage of his illness to make my escape. For this, I thought the best thing would be to confine him to the cabin; and as he promised to follow my directions implicitly, I gave this injunction the first thing, and an opportunity soon after offered. Two fishermen came on board on the following afternoon, and exchanged their cargo of fish for spirits. The evening being wet and stormy, they remained on board, and the crew inviting them to carouse, the whole were very shortly intoxicated. No further danger from the gun-boats being apprehended, the watch was neglected, and the moment I perceived this fancied state of security, hope dawned in my bosom. I knew that intoxication would make the rest sleep sound; and in order to secure the captain, in making him a mess of arrow root and wine, I infused a quantity of opiate.

At midnight all were asleep; the inclemency of the night had driven the usual sleepers on deck below, and therefore no one could see me. Not a sound was heard save the sullen roar of the waters around me, or the wind and the rain beating against the shrouds; not a star was to be seen, and the scud was flying thick and heavy. With a palpitating heart, I seized my bag that held my instruments, and in which I had secured some biscuit, and crept softly up the companion ladder, and from thence to the stern of the corsair, where the fishermen's canoe was moored. Into this I gently dropped my bag, and then, letting myself down, cut the painter, and let her drift away with the current, in order not to rouse them by any noise. When I judged myself to be out of hearing, I trimmed the canoe and set the sail, steering her in the direction, as I imagined, of the Havannah, and committing my future fate to the hands of that Providence who had hitherto preserved me.

In the morning, according to my calculation, I found myself about forty miles from the place where the pirate was at anchor, and consequently out of the reach of pursuit. The wind blew from the southwest, and what appeared to me a special Providence, continued to do so the whole day – a thing very unusual in that climate. All that day and the following night I was upon the ocean, without seeing a single vessel, & at the mercy of the waves, in a frail canoe, in which, at any other time, and under any other circumstances, I should have been afraid to trust myself. At six o'clock of the second morning of my escape, I entered the Havannah, and seeing a person walking the deck of a schooner, whose face appeared familiar to me, I ran my canoe along side, and found him to be a Captain Williams, whom I had known some years before in America. He welcomed me on board, gave me refreshments, and seeing me weak and exhausted, begged me to lie down and sleep, promising in the afternoon to introduce me to the master of a vessel, who was in want of a mate. I willingly complied with his request; for I was completely faint and exhausted with my exertions of the day and night previous.

I now imagined my sufferings were at an end; but, alas! I had yet to pass through another ordeal, as cruel and as severe as that from which I had just escaped. When I awoke from a profound sleep, in the afternoon, I found that Captain Williams had gone ashore, leaving directions with his mate where I should find him. I prevailed upon him to land me, & while proceeding up the front street, according to my directions, I met one of the men belonging to the pirate, who, the moment he saw me, ran on before till he arrived at the corner of a street, up which he turned, and I saw no more of him. I had advanced a very few paces further when the Spanish officer who had been on board the pirate, came from that direction, with a file of soldiers, and immediately arrested me as a pirate, &, charging me with having robbed him of specie to a large amount, conducted me to the governor's offices.

From thence I was taken to the prison, where I was immured in a dark dungeon, swarming with vermin, and there left without any thing to cover me, and nothing but the bare floor to lie on. My daily allowance was two ounces of meat, two of bread, and a pint of rice. In this place I was a solitary prisoner for two days, and, on the third, underwent an examination, something similar in mode to those at our own police offices, except that in this instance a judge presided. The governor's interpreter, an Irishman, was the medium through whom I was interrogated, as the judge did not understand English. This fellow, whose name was Paine, I found to be a most unprincipled and base scoundrel — a disgrace to any nation. The interrogations were put to me by this man, in English, and the answers interpreted and committed to paper in Spanish. In the course of the examination, I detailed every circumstance of my capture and forcible detention, and the cruelties I had endured; and also to different questions gave a full account of all the vessels, at the capturing of which I either assisted, or had been present. This Paine told me that Mr. Lumsden had already made every particular known. I represented to him the deplorable situation in which I was, without friends, money, or clothes, in a foreign land; but the only consolation I received was, that I should most likely be liberated after another examination, as the judge could not, under present circumstances, attach any guilt to me. My examination being concluded, I was re-conducted to my dungeon, where I was kept closely confined till the following day, and then allowed to go into a yard, containing four or five hundred prisoners of all nations, and many of the very worst description.

I had scarcely entered the place, when a sturdy looking villain came up to me & demanded my trousers, insisting that I should strip them off instantly. A Spaniard, who had formerly sailed with me in a brig, of which I was master, and who was also a prisoner, at the moment recognized me, and endeavoured to prevent him. But the sturdy villain was determined to have them, and I was actually obliged to battle, and wound him with the knife, of which I learned the use, to please the pirate, before he would forego his demand. I afterwards found that it was the practice of these fellows to rob all English and American sailors, who were unfortunate enough to become inmates of the jail, of whatever necessaries they might have.

From the Spanish sailor I received many little acts of kindness; he procured me a bedstead to lie upon, would bring me my victuals, and, in order to put me in the way of earning trifling sums, to supply my little wants, taught me to make segars, at which trade he himself earned several dollars a week, and worked for one of the largest segar shops in the town.

Five weeks elapsed, instead of two days, before I was called up for a second examination. At this I was informed that the only accusation against me was the affidavit of the Spanish officer, who was now gone to Europe; and in this he deposed, on oath, that I was one of a crew of pirates, who had robbed him of specie to a large amount. My former deposition was then read over to me; but what was my astonishment to find that every syllable of that part which related to my capture and forcible detention had been omitted, and many other things inserted that I had never uttered. I remarked this, when the Irishman, with a degree of violence, & in an authoritative tone, declared that I had never asserted any thing on the subject. A warm altercation then took place, in which I accused him as the author of my long imprisonment, and my sufferings while confined; while he, with all the voluble scurrility of his countrymen, lavished every degrading epithet on me, and concluded by a threat to represent me to the governor as a piratical scoundrel. The judge now asked this fellow what had occurred; to which he impudently replied, nothing. But, to his utter dismay, I immediately answered in Spanish, and, as well as I could, explained the whole matter in dispute.

The judge immediately answered me, and said, that, as I was a foreigner, and unacquainted with their laws, he would show me every indulgence in his power, & allow me to correct all misinterpretations; that he would then go on with my examination, and that an additional interpreter should be employed as I had requested. I was then remanded to prison, and brought up the following day. On this day, I pointed out the objectionable passages in the former deposition, all which, although strenuously opposed by this renegade Irishman, were erased from the record. One of the additional interpreters on this occasion, was Mr. Gassier, the harbour-master, who said he was ready to depose on oath that Mr. Lumsden had declared that I was forcibly detained, and that the substance of that declaration was contained in a protest deposited in one of the public notary's offices. The judge on this declared that he would examine the protest, and that if such was the fact, I should be recommended to the favourable attention of the governor. Having said this, he remanded me once more.

During the interval between this and my final examination, a serious quarrel took place among the prisoners, in which five were killed, and several wounded; and it was not until the military were called, that order could be restored. The imprecations, cries, and groans, during its continuance, were truly appalling.

After languishing several weeks in this jail, I was, at last, brought up before the governor, who sat attended by his secretary at war and two judges. Previous to being arraigned, I was asked whether I would be tried by the Spanish laws, or given up to my own government; & was informed that Captain Lillicrap, of the *Hyperion*, then in port, had demanded to have me sent to Jamaica; but that he had refused to comply with the demand, as the pirate was a Spanish vessel, and manned by Spaniards, and that, therefore, I was amenable to the laws of Spain. He said, however, that I should have my choice. I immediately begged that, as the whole of the circumstances of my case were known in the Havannah, I might be tried on the spot. The usual forms having been gone through, I entered on my defence, and recapitulated the whole of the circumstances from the capture to the moment of my escape and apprehension, dwelling forcibly upon every fact, and pointing out the injury I had sustained, not only in loss of property, but, what was far dearer to me, the loss of character; praying him to consider at the same time that I was at a distance of four thousand miles from my native country, and destitute of every means.

The governor heard me with the greatest attention, and my narrative evidently excited great interest in his mind. When I had ceased speaking, he turned round and consulted the persons upon the bench with him, and having received an affirmative answer from the judge who had examined me as to the truth of my statements, he addressed me in nearly the following words:

'In considering your case, and giving due weight to all the circumstances set forth, both in your deposition, and what you have this day laid before me, I am decidedly of opinion that you are rather an object for pity and commiseration than for prosecution. One point must, however, be enquired into, before I can decide in what way the court will dispose of you. The Admiral on the Jamaica station has made a formal application that you should be surrendered into his hands, and be at his disposal. As I know not what right he has to make this demand, or if he has the right, whether it would be consistent with the laws of Spain, and my own duty, to comply with it, I must necessarily consult with the law authorities upon the subject.

Your case shall have the earliest consideration, and be brought to as speedy a conclusion as the rules of this court will admit; but in the mean time you must remain as you are.'

I bowed when he had concluded, and was reconducted, in the usual manner, to my prison. I had been kept in painful suspense for some days, when, one forenoon, one of the judges entered the prison yard 'Your case has been decided, young man,' said he, coming up to me; 'and you are to be surrendered into the hands of the Admiral.' 'Be it so,' said I; 'my conscience acquits me of having committed any crime, & therefore I care not into whose hands I am surrendered.' 'It will be a hard case for you,' continued this upright judge, 'to be dragged to Jamaica, a prisoner, and be tried a second time. But come, you know you have been among the pirates, and have plenty of money; if you will give me and my brother judge what you have, you shall be released forthwith, and go where you please.' My blood boiled within me. 'If my liberty depends,' said I, haughtily, 'upon what money I can give, I must needs be a prisoner all my life; I never partook of the fruits of their iniquity, and have not wherewithall, at this moment, to purchase the common necessaries of life.' 'Weigh well, the proposal, young man,' cried he, with unblushing effrontery; 'my interest never fails; to it the four pirates, who were released the other day, are indebted for their safety, & from them I received four hundred doubloons.' I replied, that I had no doubloons to give him. 'Then I cannot interfere for you,' said he, coolly, and departed. The pirates whom he had liberated, had actually been convicted; and for this paltry bribe had justice been violated, and they had escaped the fate they merited.

Thus are the laws of Spain administered in the island of Cuba!

Confinement, bad diet, and agitation of mind, threw me shortly into a fever, under the effects of which I laboured for ten days, and at one time I thought it would have released me from my sufferings. But I recovered, and recovered only to meet with inhumanity where I least expected it – from an Englishman, an Admiral in His Majesty's service! I was one day called out of my bed to the gate, where I found a lieutenant of the *Sybille*, Admiral Sir Charles Rowley's flag ship, who informed me that he was going to have me liberated, and then left me.

On the following day, I found three naval officers at the gate, who, with a guard of Spanish soldiers, took me down to the beach, where the *Sybille*'s boat was in waiting. I was then, in due form, surrendered to the British government, and taken on board. What was my astonishment when I reached the deck, to hear the order that I was to be taken below, and put into double irons. This was the liberty that was promised. I was taken from where my limbs, at least, were free, to be manacled like a felon, on board of a British Admiral's flag ship. My wounds were still open, and my leg was swelled; I pointed out the excruciating pain that irons upon it would cause, and hoped that, if Sir Charles was determined to confine me, he would not torture me. The petty officers pitied me, but were obliged to obey their orders; and all they could do was to promise to report my request, & inform the surgeon. The ship's corporal shortly after returned, saying, that no orders had been given on the subject of my leg: but that the barber was to attend me, and I was then to be taken to the forecastle, and washed with cold water. Remonstrance was fruitless; I was compelled to submit to this order, and contracted so severe a cold from the effects of my submersion, that I shall never completely recover from it. This order having been complied with, to the very letter, I was taken below, and again double ironed; and, in this torture I was kept till the following day, when the Admiral visited me, accompanied by Captain Rowley.

To the latter kind, generous, and truly humane man, I feel most grateful, for alleviating my misery, and doing all in his power to render my confinement as little irksome to me as was possible. The iron from my wounded leg was removed by his interference, and the surgeon sent to dress it. From this medical man also, whose name I unfortunately have forgotten, I received the greatest kindness and attention; and I take this opportunity of expressing my gratitude to him. When the *Sybille* arrived in the higher latitudes, Captain Rowley's humanity was again conspicuously displayed. Seeing me thinly clad, he procured me warmer clothing; and, when he found that the purser had no blankets, gave me one from his own bed to cover me. During the whole voyage I was kept out of irons, with a sentry only over me, to prevent me from conversing with any one; and even this restraint would, I am sure, have been dispensed with, had he been in command.

On the arrival of the *Sybille* at the Isle of Wight, I was put in single irons. The vessel went round to Spithead, the Admiral struck his flag, and she was soon after brought to Deptford. A visible change took place as soon as the Admiral left, and my situation was rendered less irksome. In short, I cannot speak in too high terms of the kindness & humanity of all the officers, particularly Lieutenant Bennet. When the *Sybille* was taken out of commission, I was transferred to the *Aske* tender, commanded by Lieutenant Weeks, and by him conveyed on board the *Genoa* guardship, at Sheerness. Of the wanton severity and petty insults which I received from this officer, during the few hours I was in his charge, I shall say nothing. By the officers of the *Genoa* I was treated in the most humane and gentleman-like manner; and to Lieutenant Hopkins and them my warmest thanks are due. After being six days on board, I was sent up to London, in the charge of Lieutenant Hallowell, and another officer, whose name has escaped me, and was treated with uniform kindness and humanity. In London I was examined before Mr. Richbald, the presiding magistrate of the Thames Police, and by him committed to Newgate, and tried and ACQUITTED at the ensuing Admiralty Sessions. Thus has ended a series of unparalleled sufferings and persecutions, all occasioned by the obstinate infatuation of a single individual, who had not the common feelings of humanity afterwards to come forward himself in my behalf; and God forbid that such should ever fall to the lot of any man!

REPORT OF THE TRIAL OF AARON SMITH
from the *Morning Chronicle* of December 20th, 1823
HIGH COURT OF ADMIRALTY—FRIDAY.

PIRACY.

This morning the Admiralty Sessions commenced at the Old Bailey, before the Right Hon. Lord STOWELL, Mr. Baron GARROW, Mr. Justice BEST, Drs. PHILLIMORE, COOTE, SWABEY, &c.—The usual formal and preliminary business of the Court being gone through, Lord Stowell addressed the Grand Jury:

'Gentlemen of the Grand Jury.—You are met to perform a most important duty, and I am also called on to preside on the occasion; and I trust that, in our separate stations, we shall each discharge it in a proper manner. I should feel but little confidence if the result of this investigation depended on my legal knowledge. Hence it is that I feel a gratification, that I am addressing an enlightened Jury, with the nature of which many of you are familiar—namely, to investigate the several cases which will be brought before you for consideration. The nature of your duty, Gentlemen, is analogous to that you are called on to perform in courts of common law, notwithstanding there may be a difference in the facts of inquiry. There are crimes committed on the sea, which it is impossible to be committed on shore—piracy, for instance. There are also crimes committed on land, which cannot be committed at sea—house breaking &

diverse others. I am concerned to inform you, Gentlemen, that the business to come before you is of unusual extent, and some of the cases are of that grave description which will require your most minute investigation and attention. There are indictments against two persons for piracy, an offence which is held to be highly criminal in all civilised countries. Under the colour sometimes of one flag and sometimes of another, and often under the colour of existing hostilities in particular parts of the world, have those marine depredators been committing the most wanton outrages on vessels, without reference to what nation they belonged. The Americans have suffered very materially by this species of rapine and plunder. There are also two separate charges of actual murder, which require considerable attention – also another, for cutting and stabbing. Should you, after an examination of the witnesses, be of opinion that it was an act of violence without provocation, you will of course find your bill, in order that the case may be sifted to the bottom, so as it may be made apparent (should the defendant be enabled to do so) that it was only the result of pure accident. There is also an indictment for a breach of trust, where a sailor is charged with stealing rum, the particulars of which will come before you; and there are also others, as I am informed, of a minor description, the nature of which I do not know, and on which I shall not of course make any observations. You will please, Gentlemen, to withdraw, and I feel confident that you will perform your important duty with satisfaction to your consciences and justice to your country.'

At eleven o'clock the Grand Jury returned into Court, with two true bills against AARON SMITH for piracy. Whereupon Lord STOWELL, Mr. Justice BEST, Mr. Baron GARROW, and the Learned Civilians before named, took their seats on the Bench.

A true bill of indictment was also found against the prisoner for seizing the ship *Industry* on the High Seas, on the 7th of August, 1822.

AARON SMITH was then brought into Court, & placed at the bar. He appeared to be about thirty years of age, with rather an intelligent countenance. He was attired very gentlemanly in a suit of black.

The Petit Jury being sworn, the Indictment against the accused was read. It charged the prisoner, that, on the 7th of August, on the high seas, within the jurisdiction of the High Court of Admiralty of England, he the said prisoner, being a British subject, did feloniously & piratically seize a certain ship called the *Victoria*, the property of Hymen Cohen and others (the eminent West India house), and did steal and take therefrom 636 barrels of coffee, value 5,000*l*. and 100 barrels of coffee, value 1,ooo*l*., and divers other articles, the property of the said Hymen Cohen, &c. Other counts varied the form of the indictment, to which the prisoner pleaded very emphatically 'Not Guilty.'

The King's Advocate, Mr. ATTORNEY-GENERAL, Sir ROBT. GIFFORD (whose appearance in Court, after his appointment, excited some surprise), Mr. JERVIS, and Mr. EDWARD LAWES, were Counsel for the prosecution; and Mr. JOHN WILLIAMS (of Lincoln), Mr. COOPER, and another Gentleman, were Counsel for the prisoner.

Mr. EDWARD LAWES opened the pleadings, and the KING'S ADVOCATE detailed the facts of the case to the Jury. He said that the prisoner was charged with a crime more or less prevalent, according to the settled or unsettled state of civilized society. It was a long time since a similar offence had been charged against an English subject in that Court, & it would be necessary for him to say a few words upon the character of the high and capital crime which the prisoner then stood before the Court to answer. It was, in fact, a robbery on the high seas, and the offence alleged to be committed by the prisoner was against a British vessel belonging to British subjects. He should lay such evidence before them (the Jury), as would shew that the prisoner boarded a vessel called the *Victoria*, on the 7th of August, 1822, as it was sailing within seven leagues of Cuba, by a boat which was rowed from a piratical schooner, which had previously fired into the *Victoria* and brought her to; that he acted as the Commander of the boat's crew of pirates; that he was the first man who boarded the *Victoria,* and aided in taking away the property, and in using acts of great cruelty to some of the crew. The defence, he was given to understand, likely to be set up, was, that the prisoner had been himself taken by the pirates, & was acting under the force and threats of the pirates, and not of his own will and inclination. If such evidence should be offered, he believed it would be completely and satisfactorily disproved; and after some further observations, he proceeded to call his witnesses.

Edward Sadler sworn: I was last year the chief mate of the *Victoria*, a merchant ship, the property of Messrs. Cohens. (The witness mentioned the names of the proprietors severally.) The vessel sailed from London to Jamaica; Septimus Hern was the master; we took in a cargo of coffee and dye wood at Jamaica; the value of the cargo was between twenty and thirty

112

thousand pounds; we sailed from Jamaica for England on the 27th July, 1822, and on the 7th of August we lay off the island of Cuba. About nine o'clock that morning, we observed a schooner lying under the land; another brig was in company with her, but rather nearer the shore; we saw the schooner take possession of the brig after firing several guns, and then it sailed towards us; as the schooner approached the *Victoria*, a gun was fired, and we instantly hoisted the British ensign; the schooner fired a second shot, and we hove to; a boat was then put off by the schooner, and came to the *Victoria*, in which boat one man was sitting, & three were rowing; the prisoner at the bar was the person who sat in the boat; they all came on board; the prisoner entered first; they were all armed with long knifes and pistols. The prisoner had the command of the boat; his face was blacked with gunpowder, and he was so disfigured as to be completely disguised; I had previously been well acquainted with the prisoner; he was then Chief Mate of the *Latona*, and I recognised his voice though not his person; he was the first person who spoke, on the *Victoria* being boarded; he asked to see the Captain and the Second Mate, and when they appeared he ordered them into the boat, and to go on board the schooner; Captain Hern asked him what was the character of the schooner? The prisoner replied, 'you will find that out when you get on board of her,' and he then directed the Captain to take his ship's papers with him; after the Captain and Mate were in the boat, the prisoner took the command of the *Victoria*, and ordered the men to hoist the jib, and let fall the foresail, and the prisoner fired a pistol amongst the crew, as I and others were getting into the boat, to enforce his commands; we were rowed by the

113

pirates to the schooner, and brought on the quarter deck by a guard; the schooner had the United States colours flying at her mast head, and was armed with one long gun, one swivel, and three or four smaller guns; the crew of the schooner consisted of between thirty & forty men, all foreigners, chiefly Spaniards. When we went on board the Schooner, it was about one' clock in the afternoon; the brig, which had been previously captured by the Pirate, then had run into the land. I was kept on the quarter deck of the Schooner till the evening, and the *Victoria* was sailing alongside of us towards the shore. The prisoner came from the *Victoria* to the Schooner. He was dressed at that time in a boat-cloak belonging to me, which I had left on board the *Victoria*, when the Pirates forced me away. The prisoner came on the quarter-deck, and walked about it in my cloak, and said, 'how nicely it fits me.' He also took a watch out of his pocket, which I had left on board the *Victoria*, & gave it to the Captain of the Pirates, in the Schooner, and said, 'there are more watches on board.' The Captain of the Schooner gave the watch to Antonio, a Spaniard, who was one of the most active of the Pirates, to take care of it. The prisoner then ordered me to go below with Captain Hern, and we went below, and were confined in the fore-part of the hatchways all night. When we came to anchor, the Capt. of the Pirates came to the fore-hatchways, and ordered one of the 'prisoners' to come up, and one of the crew of the *Victoria*, who was brought in the boat, went up on deck, and I afterwards heard a scuffle, and the man was brought below again, very badly wounded; I saw the prisoner on the main deck of the schooner, standing amongst the crew of pirates; they were deliberating some question amongst themselves in a foreign language, and one of the chief of them went up to the prisoner and put into his hand a cutlass, and all the Pirates seemed to submit to the prisoner. After this time, the Captain of the Pirates did not exercise his power as before; but the prisoner exercised the sole and entire command of the schooner. On the same morning I saw the Pirates removing the cargo of the *Victoria* on board the schooner; the prisoner afterwards came up to me, and I and Captain Hern asked him what he intended to do with us? The prisoner said, that he intended to give us a vessel and to send us away, but every man on board had a voice, and he could do nothing of himself. He afterwards sent us on board the brig *Industry*, which had been captured the same morning as the *Victoria* was taken. The Pirates said, that we should have the *Industry* and not the *Victoria*; Captain Hern asked the prisoner for his ship's papers, and for his register and coffee certificates, and they were given to him. This witness then described the property that was taken from the *Victoria*, and stated, that after he and Captain Hern, and the crew of the *Victoria*, were put on board the *Industry*, they sailed for Kingston, Jamaica.

Cross-examined: The crew of the pirate ship were of different nations; the Captain spoke to me in English; some of the crew were Spaniards; we had a gun on board the *Victoria*, but no powder, and no chance of defending ourselves against such a force; while the prisoner was on board the *Victoria*, the schooner lay alongside of her, and could have fired into her and sunk her if she pleased, and killed all the crew.

By Mr. Baron GARROW: The prisoner was not ordered by any one to demand the ship's papers; he was by himself when he made the demand of me and the Captain.

Septimus Hern: In 1822 I was Captain of the *Victoria*, the property of Messrs. Cohens; the crew consisted of 13 persons; we were bound from London to Jamaica; on the 7th of August last year, we were in the Gulf of Florida, about seven leagues from Cuba; about one o'clock in the afternoon I saw a schooner coming towards us, towed by a boat, and I observed a boat going to and from the schooner to the brig *Industry*, which was lying a short distance from her; when the schooner was within two cables length of the *Victoria* she fired a gun at her, and from the sound, I believe it was loaded with shot; a boat was then put off from the schooner, in which were four men, three of them were rowing, and one of them, a young man, was standing upright in the aft of the boat, while they rowed to the *Victoria*; he came on board first, and the other three followed him; his face was blacked, and I cannot say that it was the prisoner at the Bar; I saw the prisoner at the Thames Police-office, and then stated, that there was a strong resemblance between him and the man who commanded the boat's crew that boarded the *Victoria*; but I could not swear positively to his identity; when the party came on board, they were armed with one or two pair of pistols each, which hung in belts thrown over their shoulders, and also cutlasses and knives; the person I take to be the prisoner said, that he wanted the Captain and the second mate; I and the second mate went up to him, and I asked him what he wanted? He said, that I should know when I got on board the schooner; I asked if I should take my papers with me? He said, that I might do so, and ordered me into the boat; at that time the prisoner ordered the sails of the *Victoria* to be lowered, & fired a pistol amongst the crew, to compel them to obey his order with promptitude, and I and the second mate, with three seamen and one passenger, went in the boat to the schooner. The person I suppose to be the prisoner, on our leaving the *Victoria*, took the command of her. I saw him afterwards come on board the schooner, but he did not then converse with me; he wore at that time a large tartan cloak; this was the morning after the capture. During the night we were confined in the schooner, below, and two centinels were placed over us. The young man who first boarded the *Victoria* [here the witness alluded to the prisoner], said he was sorry for my case, and I told him that it was in his power to relieve me. He said that he had been forced into the piratical schooner himself, when second mate of a merchant vessel sailing from Kingston to London. I then asked him to give me up the brig *Victoria* to sail away; he replied that he could not, for the crew of the schooner had made up their minds to keep it and to give up the *Industry*. I then asked him for the ship's register, to enable my employers to recover of the London under-writers, and he gave it to me. I also asked for some clothes, for we were in great distress for apparel, and he said that he could not give them, and that we might think ourselves well off if we escaped with our lives.

— Oldham: I was a seaman on board the *Victoria*; I saw the prisoner on 7th Aug. 1822, board the brig, in a boat with three seamen, who came from a privateer. He ordered the Captain, the second mate, and three seamen into a boat, and sent them on board the schooner. He continued on board the *Victoria*, and assumed the command. He ordered the jib and the fore-sail to be lowered, and swore at the crew, if they did not do it quickly, he would shoot them, & fired a pistol amongst them. We had one seaman, named Dean, on board the *Victoria*, the prisoner cut him on the head with a cutlass, and swore he would cut him down if Dean did not direct the ship in its due course after the brig. Dean afterwards went down the fore-castle to get a *chaw* of tobacco. On his return the prisoner struck him with his cutlass on the neck and shoulders, which were sorely injured; Dean cried for mercy, and then he was ordered to go aft by the prisoner. Another of the crew was afterwards struck by the prisoner with a cutlass, for not steering to please him, and another man was afterwards struck in the same manner by him without any cause whatever, and the prisoner fired a pistol at the man's head, and told him, that if he fired again he would do it to some purpose. The prisoner had two pistols, which he fired twice each; while we were hoisting the foretop-mast and studding sail, he fired his pistol at the crew, & afterwards ordered the steward to give us a glass of brandy each. A glass was offered to me, but I refused to drink it; and the prisoner said, who is it that refuses to drink a glass of brandy? He afterwards asked me what countryman I was, and if I was an American? I said no, I was an Englishman. He asked what countrymen the captain and mate were, and if they were allowed private trading? I said they were allowed to trade privvately, & that they were Englishmen, and that the Captain lived in Newport-street, London. He then asked me if Dean was an Englishman? I told him that he was an Irishman; he replied, 'then he is none the better for that.' The prisoner ordered me to keep the ship pumped, as it leaked; and when I said the

118

Captain lived in Newport-street, London, he replied, 'Don't tell me of London, I know nothing of it.' He asked me of what the ship's cargo consisted, and I told him; he said I must do the same as if the Captain was on board, for he was the Captain then. It began to rain and became squally, and the prisoner put on a pair of the Captain's shoes, and the second mate's boat cloak. The prisoner ordered all the arms that were on board to be brought on deck and shewn to him; they consisted of three cutlasses and two guns, and the prisoner wanted to ascertain if they were loaded: he found they were not. He saw an American schooner heave in sight, and the prisoner went aloft with his telescope, and on coming down he ordered the long-boat to be launched, and four of the men to be ready to tow the *Victoria* a-head. The wind blew fresh, and we got ahead of the American schooner; we kept a heavy press of sail, and we thought at times the mast would be blown away. We were afterwards put on board the *Industry*. When I was going over the side of the *Victoria* I was told I must join the piratical schooner, but I went to the *Industry*.

Cross-examined by Mr. Cooper: The schooner was within pistol-shot of the *Victoria* all the time, and could have fired into us and killed us had we attempted to escape. When the American schooner was in sight, the *Victoria* might, I think, then have been dropped for it to come up, if the prisoner had wished to relieve us. I am sure it was an American schooner that chased us.

By Mr. Baron Garrow: When the prisoner descended from the top, after spying the American, he said nothing, except ordering out the long boat to tow the ship, if the weather should calm.

Thomas Davis: Was boatswain of the *Victoria*.

This witness corroborated the former witnesses, as to the prisoner boarding the brig, and continued : — The prisoner ordered Dean, a seaman, to the wheel, and other sailors were directed to hoist the jib. While Dean was steering the ship, the prisoner struck him on the head with a cutlass, which inflicted a wound three or four inches long. The prisoner ordered Hownam, the cook, to kill six fowls for dinner. Dean had done nothing to deserve the violent treatment of the prisoner. The prisoner then sent Dean aft, and ordered Lewis, another sailor, to the wheel, and he not pleasing him, received a blow on the head with the prisoner's telescope; I was then ordered by the prisoner to steer after the Pirate schooner, and he swore if I did not steer to his liking he would fire at me, and while I was steering he fired his pistol at my head; the pistol was loaded, for the ball whistled by my head; he afterwards threatened to run me through the body with his sword if I did not clear the wheel ropes, which had got foul, and he attempted to do it, but the Spaniard, Antonio, prevented him, and said to him, 'Don't be so cruel, he can't steer the ship while the wheel ropes are foul.' Wm. Lewis, a seaman, went to the wheel after me. When the prisoner returned from aloft, after spying the American schooner, he said, 'I think the schooner coming towards us is a rogue,' meaning an enemy, and then he ordered the long boat out, to enable them to get away if becalmed; the prisoner addressed this language to Antonio the Spaniard; they spoke part in English and part in Spanish; I understand Spanish a little; the prisoner said that he thought the schooner that was in sight was an American which he had seen some days before; the Spaniard said that he thought so too; when the prisoner left the ship he had Mr. Sadler's cloak on.

Cross-examined by Mr. WILLIAMS: The prisoner was three yards from me when he fired the pistol; he had two pistols; I can't say that both were loaded; there was nothing between him and me; he could have blown out my brains if he had chosen; he was angry with me because I did not steer the ship in the due course; all the Spaniards spoke very bad English; the prisoner spoke good English; the squall had begun when the prisoner put the mate's cloak on. — Re-examined: At the time the American schooner hove in sight the pirate Schooner was two miles behind the *Victoria*; I think the prisoner might have escaped from the pirate on board of the American schooner if he had pleased: it was a dark and squally night, and I cannot speak positively.

John Holman, the cook on board the *Victoria*, cor-roborated the above evidence, and said that he killed and dressed six fowls by order of the prisoner, who partook of them along with the pirates. — Mr. Baron GARROW: Prisoner at the bar, the evidence for the prosecution is now closed; the rules of this Court do not allow your Counsel to address the Jury in your behalf; but you may do so if you think proper.

The prisoner took from his pocket a written paper, which he read to the Jury; but was so affected with his situation, that for some time he could not give utter-ance to a single word. The defence was well drawn up, and was to the following effect:—He was mate on board a merchant ship, called the *Zephyr*, in June 1822; and when sailing off Cape Antonio, the *Zephyr* was boarded by a Spanish privateer, and he and other per-sons were taken out of the ship, on board the piratical schooner. He was carried forcibly away by the pirates,

and was obliged to work the ship. He underwent the
most shocking tortures to force him to navigate the
vessel, and to assist them in their wicked enterprise.
He had been confined to a solitary dungeon, lashed to
the vessel and flogged, powder was placed at his feet
and set fire to, and the flesh blown off his legs, and his
clothes consumed because he merely evinced some
objection to join a diabolical crew of miscreants
against the property and lives of his own countrymen.
All that he had done had been from fear; his spirit had
been broken by the cruelties practised upon him by
the most diabolical monster that ever was in human
shape—the Captain of the Pirates; and the circumstances which had been detailed by the witnesses as
acts of cruelty, were done by him to save himself from
further torture. When he fired the pistol, as it had
been stated at the ship's crew, he took care to fire in a
direction that should injure no one and also when he
fired by the side of the head of the man steering the
Victoria he could, if he had chosen, have shot him
dead. This appearance of cruelty was assumed on his
part, to deceive the Pirates; and he declared to God
most solemnly, that he did not intend to cut the man
on the head, for he struck him with the flat part of the
cutlass. He called upon the Jury to weigh well his case
before they consigned him to an ignominious death;
for though there might be appearances of guilt against
him, yet God, the searcher of all hearts knew, that he
was forced to do what he had done: and that he had no
opportunity of escaping from the Pirate. He had
always enjoyed a good reputation, and never received
a penny, or the value of it, from the Pirates; and when
he was taken, he had only two half-crowns about his
person, and his dress was most wretched, which must,

in some degree, convince the Jury that he had no share in the Piracy. He was on his way to England to join his friends, and to marry one that he loved dearer than his life, when his hopes were blasted by his detention by the Pirates, and his sufferings had been almost beyond human endurance. While he had been under the lash of the monster, the Captain of the Pirates, he had repeatedly called upon him in mercy to put him to death, and his answer had been, 'No; I want your services, and I will have them.' Such was his situation when the Captain of the Pirates ordered him to board the *Victoria*, and had he followed his commands, not a soul would have been left alive on board. He again appealed to his Maker that he was not a voluntary actor in the scenes described by the witnesses, and trusted the Jury, by their verdict, would acquit him.

John Webster: I was on board the *Zephyr* in June, 1822, at the time she was boarded by a Privateer. The prisoner was a mate on board the ship; one of the Pirates who boarded her was named Antonio; he appeared to have the command of the Privateer; the prisoner and Captains Lumsden and Camphine were on board the *Zephyr*, and were removed by the Pirates to their schooner: we were bound for England; I never heard of the prisoner having sustained an injury of his legs at the time he was taken by the Pirates from the *Zephyr*; I am the son of one of the owners of the *Zephyr*.

Cross-examined.—This happened off Cuba in May or June 1822. I have seen Captain Lumsden and spoken to him to-day; he and Captain Camphine were brought back to the *Zephyr*, after being detained all night by the pirates; the prisoner did not return to the *Zephyr*; the pirates suffered the *Zephyr* to proceed next day, and Captains Lumsden and Camphine came home in her.

Captain Kelly sworn: I was master of the *Harrington* in 1821; the prisoner was my first mate. In 1821 I sailed to the Bermudas, intending to return direct to England; I parted with the prisoner at the Bermudas on account of his wish to return to England, and I recommended him to Captain Lumsden; the prisoner's conduct was always irreproachable, and I would have kept him if I could; I have so good an opinion of him that I would take him now; when he left me his legs and feet were sound.

Thos. Merrick, a seaman on board the *Zephyr*, corroborated the evidence of the first witness for the defence, as to the prisoner being taken by the pirates, which was corroborated by other seamen on board the same vessel.

Mr. Holmes, the Deputy Surgeon of Newgate, and another Medical Gentleman, deposed to the fact of the prisoner's legs being injured, apparently by the explosion of gunpowder.

Miss Sophia Knight, a female of considerable personal attractions, was called. She was exceedingly agitated, and the prisoner burst into tears as she entered the witnesses box; she said, I have been intimately acquainted with the prisoner for more than three years. This letter (a letter put into her hands) is from him; it is the last that ever reached me. It is dated Oct. 1821. After the date of the letter, I expected, on the prisoner arriving in England, that I should become his wife; it was so arranged [here she wept, & the prisoner appeared deeply affected].

Mr. John Smith: Is a brother of the prisoner; is an officer in his Majesty's navy; the prisoner possessed a considerable sum of money, and it was arranged that he should quit the sea, and he was to have returned to England in 1822, to be married to the young lady last examined.

Mr. William Henry, a rope-maker, of Limehouse, had known the prisoner for four years, and believed him to be as incapable of committing the offence he stood charged with as the most honourable minded person in Court.

Mr. George Watson, a gentleman who had known the prisoner some years, gave him the highest character for honesty and humanity. — Mr. Buthroy, of Limehouse, and other persons, spoke to the same effect. — John M'Kinnon sworn: I was steward of the *Industry* when she was captured by the pirate schooner. The prisoner and five or six foreigners came on board when she was taken. A general order of command was given to the crew of the *Industry* to go on board the schooner. I did not see the prisoner give any command whatever. The prisoner appeared to be acting under the pirates' command. I saw the captain of the pirates when I first went alongside the schooner. Captain Cooke was Captain of the *Industry*, and he was taken on board the piratical schooner. — The captain of the privateer struck Captain Cooke with his cutlass, & threatened to put him to death, and the prisoner interfered, and I think saved him from death. The prisoner touched the Captain of the pirate on the shoulder, and told him to desist from striking Captain Cooke, and the pirate threatened the prisoner, and struck his sword at him, ordered him below, & he went below. After I was on board the piratical schooner, the *Victoria* was attacked and taken. We were compelled to work the pirate's guns, and get the

125

powder to fire on the *Victoria*, and were kept in duress during the time by the pirates *whopping* us on the head with a rope's end [laughter]. Captain Cooke was ordered into a boat by the pirate captain; and after he entered it, the pirate captain aimed a pistol at his head, and threatened to shoot him, but the prisoner, finding his interference of no effect, urged the crew to save Captain Cooke, and they pushed the pirate back, and prevented his firing. I saw the prisoner come on board from the *Victoria*, with a tartan cloak. The pirate captain said to him 'You rascal, why did you not bring more clothes?' I was down below great part of the night, with the prisoner, not confined. The rest of the crew of the *Industry* were confined. — Mr. Williams: Did the prisoner complain to you of his being under restraint, & of his bad treatment, I do not ask the exact words? — The ATTORNEY-GENERAL objected to the question; it was argued, and after the Judges had delivered their opinion, the examination continued.

Witness: The prisoner appeared to be under compulsion and restraint; he told me that he would use every means to effect his escape from the pirates, but he was fearful he should not effect it. While I and the prisoner were kept below, the pirates were on deck.

Cross-examined by the ATTORNEY-GENERAL I cannot say who had the command of the party that boarded the *Industry*; the prisoner was the first that went on board; he addressed the Captain of the *Industry*; he had a belt over his shoulders, and was armed with a brace of pistols and a cutlass; the prisoner was the only one who spoke English; we all messed with the Pirate's crew. When the Captain of the Pirates swore he would shoot Captain Cooke, the prisoner begged the crew to interfere in his behalf; at this time he so interfered, he spoke to the crew from the cabin, which he could see through a skylight. I did not see the prisoner after his return from the *Victoria* produce a watch; I cannot say that the prisoner had the command of the party who took the *Victoria*; I have no opinion on the subject.

Re-examined by Mr. WILLIAMS: I am 19 years of age; I am not connected with the prisoner in any way.

David Hayes, the Captain of a ship on board of which the prisoner was mate, gave him the best of characters.

About 20 most respectable witnesses were then called to character. They all of them had known the prisoner for years, and described him as a very humane and respectable man, possessing a nice sense of honour, and manners the most gentlemanly, and utterly incapable of the offence imputed to him.

The ATTORNEY-GENERAL called Captain Cooke, the Master of the *Industry*, to contradict the witness M'Kinnon. Mr. WILLIAMS objected, and said that he ought to have been called in the first instance, before the prisoner was put on his defence. This was ably urged also by Mr. COOPER; but over-ruled by the Judges.

Capt. Cooke examined by Mr. JERVIS: I was Captain of the *Industry*, and was boarded on the 7th of August, 1822, by a boat from the pirate schooner, about eleven o'clock in the forenoon: Smith was one of them, and he appeared to have the command; he got on board first, and ordered two centinels on the hatchways; he was armed with one or two braces of pistols, and a cutlass. On his ordering the crew of the pirate's boat, they obeyed him. He asked me if I had any passengers on board? I said I had one. He ordered my Mate to go on board the schooner with my papers; and we did so. Before the *Industry* was taken, it was fired at by the Pirate, for six hours, and the prisoner said to me 'Curse your blood, why did you not heave to sooner?' I told him that I thought I knew him; he said I was mistaken; I told him that I had seen him in London, and his name was Smith. He said, 'my name is not Smith,' and he drew his sword, which he menaced to either his or my crew. His face was blacked, and the impression on my mind was that he had done it to disguise himself. My boat was not in a good condition, and I requested to go in his boat; he said I might if I pleased. Eight of my crew went on board the pirate schooner, and the prisoner left two of my crew on board the *Industry*. The *Industry* was a quarter of a mile off the pirate schooner when we entered the boat. On my entering the pirate ship, the Captain cut and slashed at me with his sword till it broke; the crew interfered to save me. I did not see the prisoner interfere. If he had, I think I must have seen him. I was then ordered into a boat, to tow it, but I did not understand the order, and being afraid they wanted to throw me into the water, I refused to go; and I asked for a hat to put on my head, as the sun was vertical; the Pirate Captain fired a pistol at my head, and struck me with a cutlass, but the crew took it from him. I called to the prisoner, and said, 'Smith, will you see me murdered?'

Smith did not reply, nor did he interfere. I do not think that he durst interfere. The Captain was a savage, ferocious fellow. I afterwards saw the prisoner and the Captain laughing and talking together; I do not know that the prisoner, when he was on board the *Victoria*, had an opportunity of sailing away, and escaping, if he had pleased. When I was in the boat the Captain kept

128

a musket pointed at me. I then called to Smith to save me from being murdered. The crew were also savage-looking men, but their dispositions were not so brutal as the Captain's. — Cross-examined: The Captain had abundantly the appearance of a ferocious fellow.

By the Prisoner: Before the capture of the *Victoria* by the pirates, were not your crew compelled to work the pirate's guns? — A. Yes; they were obliged to man them, and the pirates stood over them with drawn swords during the time.

The prisoner again begged to address the Court. He declared that he was compelled by the most cruel torture inflicted upon him by the savagest monster that ever lived to do what he had done, and made a most pathetic appeal to the Jury.

Mr. Baron GARROW, in his address to the Jury, said, that the offence of which the prisoner stood charged was one of the highest character in civilized society, and it was of the last importance that such a practice should be suppressed and the offender punished; it was also of the most serious importance to the prisoner, as well as to society, and he (being a British subject) would have the advantage of a British Jury. The Learned Judge then described the nature and character of the offence, and adverted to the system of piracy recently practised near the West India Islands, & having recapitulated the evidence, called upon the Jury to convict the prisoner if they were satisfied of his guilt; and if they could possibly entertain a doubt of it to acquit him.

The Jury returned a verdict of — Not Guilty.

The prisoner was arraigned *pro forma* on the second indictment, and acquitted.

POSTSCRIPT
by Robert S. Redmond

One
THE WANTED MAN

Aaron tells us how, sometimes, he feared for his fate had the pirate schooner been attacked by a Royal Navy or American man of war. It is easy to understand that, if he had been discovered among a pirate crew, a naval captain might have found his story far from credible. On the other hand, he was confident that if he could escape, all he had to do was to find his way back to England and he would be safe. It cannot have occurred to him that he was regarded as a pirate of whom the Royal Navy wished to make an example. After all, Lumsden had put in at Havana and reported on his capture. Surely, he would have the sympathy of his fellow countrymen.

Several times in his own account, too, we read criticism of both British and American navies for their schooners with shallow draught.

When he was back in England, Aaron tells us he was informed that Captain Septimus Hearn of *Vittoria* (not *Victoria* as reported in *Morning Chronicle*) had been put aboard a man of war. Why, therefore, did not that ship start a search for pirates at once? He obviously did not realise what Septimus Hearn and his crew had told the Royal Naval Captain. It was, nevertheless, as a result of that encounter that the Royal Navy began to look for him. He was regarded as a renegade – an Englishman who merited the disgust and animosity of all honest seafarers. He had to be brought to justice and to his richly deserved end on the gallows as soon as possible.

Industry met HMS *Carnation* while the latter was 'cruising between the Bay of Honde and Cape San Antonio, westward of the Island of Cuba' on 12th August 1822. Her captain Commander Edward Walcot reported to the Admiralty in a lengthy document giving the full story, as told to him, of 'the capture of two British merchant vessels westward of the Island of Cuba'. This report is now in the Public Record Office in London (reference ADM1/2721 17657). Walcot considered it his duty to enclose '...the depositions made before me by the master of the captured brig *Vittoria* who, together with his crew, I received on board 10th instant off the Havana from the brig *Industry*'. It was from what he was told by Hearn and others that Walcot based the report which created Aaron's awful reputation.

He tells how, after the capture, both *Industry* and *Vittoria* were anchored below the Bay of Honde. The man described as the leader of the pirates came on deck and expressed his determination to murder the masters and crews of both vessels. This was not acceptable to the pirates and a scuffle ensued in which the 'leader' had been killed. We have, of course, heard about this from Aaron, but what is, perhaps, surprising is that Walcot was given to understand that this 'leader' was succeeded by 'an Englishman named Smith' who clearly had great influence among the pirates.

Walcot goes on to report that *Industry* had been carrying a cargo of rum from Jamaica to St Thomas's, while *Vittoria* had been loaded with coffee from Jamaica for London. She had sailed on 7th July. *Industry* had been 'liberated' with both crews while *Vittoria* had been taken by a prize crew towards Cape San Antonio, 'to the westward of which lies a creek which from experience is known to have been made use of by pirates,' (This would be Rio Medias, the home of Seraphina and her magistrate father). Readers of *Treasure Island* will be interested to learn that the rum from *Industry* had far less appeal than the coffee from *Vittoria*. It was coffee that sold well in the market in Havana.

Commander Walcot gives us a full description of the schooner and the pirates as explained to him. The vessel was of about 70 tons with a crew of thirty-five men. He tells us that two of the pirates were English, but only Aaron Smith is named. In addition, there were three Dutchmen from *Prevoyante* and the remainder were Spanish Creole. *Prevoyante* was the Dutch ship taken by the pirates just before *Industry* and *Vittoria*.

Walcot tells us nothing about that other Englishman, but he describes Aaron in some detail. He had been told he stood five feet eight inches tall, with a dark complexion, a scar on his right cheek and his face masked with gunpowder. He was very slender. Someone had told him that:

> Smith, by his own statement to which little credit is due, had been taken a month previous in a merchant brig from Kingston for England; that he had further stated himself to be serving unwillingly. The name of the brig from which he had been taken, he did not mention, but the master of which had been murdered by the pirates.

It is fair to assume that Aaron had told someone aboard *Vittoria* that *Zephyr* had put in at Havana and that the pirate had sent Stromeda to Havana to murder Lumsden. If so, his object would have been to give credence to his story. It is a pity that he did not make himself clear instead of prejudicing his own position.

Walcot goes on in a manner serving to answer most of Aaron's strictures against the Royal Navy and his ideas about the reluctance of Captains to pursue Pirates as he thought they should have done. He reports that *Carnation* had sailed out of Havana on the morning he had met *Industry* and that he was bound for Jamaica. He had entered Havana on the 1st of the month with treasure collected at Vera Cruz, Tampico and Campeche. He was there to receive money for Jamaican merchants. His orders from the Commander-in-Chief, Rear Admiral Sir Charles Rowley, were to take station off Cape San Antonio on his return from Jamaica for the 'protection of the trade' for a few days. As a result of what he had now heard from *Industry*, he decided to keep close in shore in order to assist any merchant ship rounding Cape San Antonio. He knew that another Royal Naval man-of-war would be leaving Havana on 13th or 14th and that she would be able to provide the necessary protection after that.

Here we see the Royal Naval answer to Aaron's complaints and what he describes as a dereliction of duty by ships carrying specie and making direct voyage without attending to the need to protect mercantile property. Aaron used strong language about both British and American Navies, but we can now see that had *Carnation* met the pirate while a merchant vessel of any nationality was under attack, Commander Walcot would have gone into action despite his cargo of treasure. At the same time, his report adds that prudence dictated against trying to proceed inside the Colorado shoal in Carnation without a pilot in view of her draught. Nor would he make any serious effort which would put his ship in danger and in violation of Spanish territorial waters. He makes it clear that had he felt able to do this, it would have been 'with great pleasure'.

It is also reasonable to assume that if he could have found the pirate schooner and arrested Aaron Smith, it would have been to his credit with his Admiral.

Walcot includes in his report the depositions of Edward Sadler, mate of *Vittoria* and of Captain Septimus Hearn the master. Since both statements match closely the evidence they gave at the Old Bailey and which was reported in the *Morning Chronicle*, there is no point in repeating them here. They were, nevertheless, enough to make the Royal Navy determined to arrest Aaron as quickly as possible. The prima facie evidence branded him as a notorious criminal. There is no reason to doubt that Commander Walcot would wish to be scrupulously fair in spite of a natural animosity towards an Englishman turned pirate. It is, therefore, sad that he did not also take statements from others including John McKinnon, steward of *Industry* who appeared for the defence at the Old Bailey. Perhaps if he had done so, he might have been less inclined to dismiss what Aaron was reported to have said about his own situation. He did not, of course, speak to anyone from *Industry* at all. He allowed her to proceed on her way, relying entirely on the crew of *Vittoria*.

Commander Walcot, for some reason not explained, addressed his report directly to the Admiralty and not to his Commander-in-Chief at Jamaica though he trusted 'that my Lords Commissioners of the Admiralty will consider (me) justified in this direct communication' . We do not know how long it took for the document to reach London. Nor can we say whether the Admiral in Jamaica approved or disapproved of being by-passed in this way.

We do know that Rear Admiral Sir Charles Rowley had been active for some months in pressing the Spanish authorities for action against pirates in general. He was not a man to stand for any nonsense and must have been one of the Royal Navy's strictest and harshest commanders. He was a friend of the Duke of Clarence, later to become King William IV, and had a record of the most violent temper with liberal use of the lash in enforcing discipline in any ship under his command. The attitude of Spanish officialdom, therefore, must have tried his patience which was always on a short fuse. He was obviously a very different character from his Flag Captain, Joseph R. Rowley who was his nephew.

It is probable that Aaron Smith had left the pirate schooner within days of the capture of *Industry* and *Vittoria*. Yet on 3rd October 1822, the Admiral wrote from 'His Britannic Majesty's Ship Sybille at Port Royal Harbour, Jamaica' to His Excellency Don P. Kindelan, Acting Captain General of Cuba (Public Record Office ADM1 272):

> ... I am led to hope that from the terms of your communication of 9th August that the parties concerned in the outrages upon ... *Zephyr* and now the more recent instance of *Industry* and *Vittoria* have already been taken and brought to justice. Should that unfortunately not be the case, I have to draw your Excellency's attention to the details of the capture of the latter vessel, her cargo being coffee and of that magnitude that it is impossible it could have been landed in the Island of Cuba without knowledge of many individuals and if effective measures are now taken by the subordinate officers under Your Excellency – 'Smith' cannot escape them and it is probable that other Englishmen detained may be recovered.

The Admiral was not without his sources of intelligence and this letter makes it as clear as diplomatic protocol would allow, that he had a good idea that, first, the Don himself was lining his own pocket in league with pirates and also that it was highly probable that Aaron Smith was in Havana being held in the hope of a bribe or 'ransom'.

Captain Theed of HMS *Tamar* reported (Admi1 275) early in October:

> During my stay in Havana, I endeavoured to collect every information which I could relating to the acts of piracy said to have been committed in the vicinity of Cuba. The lethargy or connivance, I know not which, of the Spanish Authorities exceeds almost all belief. The chief rendezvous of the pirates has been the Bay of Honde, not

139

more than 40 miles from Havana.

By 16th March 1823 (Admi1 5085) things seem to have been moving. Captain J.W. Lillicrap, aboard HMS *Hyperion* at Havana wrote to Don P. Kindelan showing that he knew Aaron Smith was in custody and arguing that, as a British subject, accused of piracy against British ships, he must be handed over for trial by a British court:

> I am to thank Your Excellency for the communication in which you have done me the honour to make known to me in your despatch of this morning in reply to mine of 13th instant respecting the person of the Englishman Smith. Your Excellency will no doubt remember the anxiety expressed in the Despatch of Rear Admiral Sir C. Rowley dated 3rd October last for the apprehension of this very person in which he calls Your Excellency's attention to the atrocities committed on *Industry* and *Vittoria* in particular, and of aggression and piracy in which the above named person has been engaged appear to have been committed on British commerce alone and which is the ground work of my motive for claiming him, as it will in all probability lead to a discovery and detection of other individuals who have been or are engaged in such unlawful practices. In reference to that part of the Auditor of War's opinion as to his being classed with and considered an insurgent and subject to the laws of that nation in which he has committed acts of violence – I acknowledge to be most just but considering him in a worse light, that of a pirate and enemy to all mankind. I repeat my hopes that he may be given up to be tried by the Tribunals and laws of that country which he acknowledges himself to be a native of.

Lillicrap wrote again on 20th April (same reference):

> I have the honour to enclose to Your Excellency a copy of my letter to His Excellency the Commandant General of

140

Marine ... and to repeat to Your Excellency my hope that
Smith, the Englishman accused of piracy may be given up
upon the ground which I stated in my letter of 16th Ultimo,
as it will most decidedly lead to the detection of others and
become of general good to all. I have directed Captain
Wigston of HBM ship *Scout*, under my orders to consult
with Your Excellency on the subject and who will take
charge of Smith should Your Excellency feel disposed to
direct his being delivered up.

Yet it took another month before Aaron was on his way
home 'manacled like a felon'. The Captain's Log of
HMS *Sybille* for 3rd May 1823 tells us (Adm51 3465):

> Moored in Havana Harbour PM. Received Aaron Smith
> from the Spanish prison for a passage to England to be tried
> for piracy.

The ship's muster book records that Aaron was discharged to HMS *Genoa* on 28th June 1823 and that
vessel's muster book shows he was handed over to
Thames Police on 29th June.

HMS *Sybille* was a fifth rate, or frigate with 44
guns. She was French built having been captured in
the Mediterranean in 1794. At that time, she had been
known as *La Sybille*.

Being relatively small for a flagship, she could
never have provided for a comfortable passage for a
man in irons – even without the brutal Admiral who
was returning home after completing his tour in the
Jamaica station.

Anyone who has visited HMS *Victory* at
Portsmouth knows something of the conditions in a
warship of that time. But *Victory* was one of the biggest
warships afloat.

A great deal had happened between Aaron's capture

aboard *Zephyr* on 7th July 1822 and 3rd May 1823 when he was taken to HMS *Sybille*. Had he known what was going on, he might have been less surprised by his reception.

Two
THE END OF THE PIRATE SCHOONER

Commander Walcot, in his report about his meeting with *Industry* goes some way to answering Aaron's criticisms of both British and American navies and what he called their neglect of attention to the pirate menace. If Aaron had known the final fate of that schooner in which he had been captive, he may have shown a greater understanding of the true position and been less critical of men who were doing their duty under difficult circumstances.

Walcot expressed his reservations against entering Cuban territorial waters lest a diplomatic incident might be created. This was completely justified.

Cuba was a principal trading post in the transatlantic slave trade. Spanish traders objected strongly to the manner in which Britain had taken it upon herself to enforce the law. To put it bluntly, they thought the Royal Navy should mind its own business and not interfere in what they thought legitimate commercial activity. It was also clear that piracy was equally acceptable to Cuban officials and entry into their territorial waters would cut their profits. Walcot had good reason to believe a naval officer might find himself under arrest and in a Cuban gaol for illegal violation of territorial waters. While, of course, he would have been released after strong diplomatic pressure, such an experience would hardly further an otherwise promising career.

Nevertheless, once the Royal Navy was aware of a British subject, answerable to the laws of England being involved in the heinous crime of piracy against British ships, British people and British property, an all out search would begin and every effort would be made to bring the renegade to justice. While the Spaniards might not like this, they could not very well protest. After all, the action would have been taken to help the forces of law and order – whatever their views on that score. Moreover, after the many attacks on British merchant ships, the Captain General, Don Kindelan was finding himself and his whole administration under heavy pressure from Admiral Rowley and, probably, others to act against pirates. He could hardly turn down 'assistance' from a 'friendly' power. There was, too, always the possibility of an ultimatum from London or Washington to Madrid. That could have threatened the job of every senior colonial civil servant in the island.

In the letters and dispatches available to us, we read of Royal Navy ships putting in at Havana for water. This was a perfectly legitimate purpose, but it did give officers the opportunity of seeing cargoes, particularly coffee, on sale in the Havana market and, maybe, learning more about the ways of the pirates.

So it was that HMS *Speedwell*, a tiny Naval tender, played a leading role in ending the career of Aaron's captor. She did it with the help of USS *Peacock*, an American brig of war.

In a letter to the Admiralty, dated 11th November 1822, Sir Charles Rowley enclosed a copy of a report to him from William Geary, Master's Mate in charge of *Speedwell*. No one could ever accuse the Admiral of wearing his heart on his sleeve. He was famous for being stinting with praise and swift to condemn. Yet, in this letter (ADM1/273 174996), we read that:

> The general conduct of this petty officer has merited my approbation and he is the individual in whose favour I transmitted to their Lordships in my letter No 23 of the 12th February last flattering testimonials from General Grant, the House of Assembly and Chambers of Commerce of New Providence.

Geary was certainly in everyone's good books. Yet his ship was so tiny that it did not rate a commissioned officer in command. At Havana on 7th October 1822, Geary made a full written report to Sir Charles. It told how, on 29th September, he was cruising about four leagues to the West of the Bay of Honde and some two miles outside the reef. He goes on:

> At 12 noon, I observed two schooners running towards the westward. I stood for them, keeping between them and the land and as much disguised as possible, but they soon discovered what we were and pushed over a part of the reef into shallow water. I kept on until we came abreast of where they got over, but found too little water to attempt to follow. Seeing they were full of men, I hoisted my colours and fired at headmast which was instantly returned

by both, each at the same time hoisting a Red Flag.

I then hove to, with a determination to keep them where they were until I could devise some plan of attack, as from their great superiority of men it would have been useless to attempt anything with my boats. After some time, I filled and made sail to try and decoy them out, but without success. They only commenced firing again, but without effect as we could not close. At 3 p.m. we observed another sail in the same direction we had at first seen them and thinking her to be a companion, made sail in chase, but which proved to be the United States ship *Peacock*.

The Officer who came on board informed me that they had chased three schooners in the morning, one of which they took, but the others escaped inshore which must have been the pirates we had forced into the Reef. We formed a plan of co-operation with *Peacock*, for *Speedwell* and a schooner she had in company, to keep inshore that night and all her boats with the schooner and ours to attack them in the morning.

Our boats accordingly went inside in the morning and I am happy to inform you, Sir, succeeded in capturing the Pirates [he means the ships, not the men] with two smaller vessels partly loaded with coffee which we found scuttled, saved the cargo and set fire to it. We also burned a large schooner they had run aground, together with the whole of their settlements, houses, huts and everything which appeared to belong to the pirates, but I am sorry to say every man escaped on shore. There was strewn about on shore all kinds of plundered property that can be imagined and seemed to have been wantonly destroyed, but principally coffee marked on the bags TNT, supposed of the *Vittoria* whose Bill of Lading was found on board one of the pirate schooners, with *Industry's* clearance and letters of the *Jane*, *Anne*, *Retrench*, and *Mary Ann* and a French ship. Some coffee of the same mark has been selling in Havana and known to be Jamaica produce.

The Governor and Admiral are highly pleased at our proceedings and success and have dispatched since a squadron of gunboats and other vessels to that part of the coast.

Captain Cassis of *Peacock* has manned and sent the prizes to America for condemnation and has expressed his acknowledgement of our success in a letter which I have the honour to enclose.

Geary then shows the natural reaction of a master's mate. He was worried lest he be held responsible and charged for damage to the vessel under his command. He would know the harsh ways of the Royal Navy and of a 'difficult' Admiral. He continued:

> I am concerned to be obliged to inform you, Sir, that in endeavouring to get in after the pirates and cover the Boats, we got ashore on the reef, but by the prompt and ready assistance of the boats of the *Peacock*, soon got off after starting our water and by lightening her a little and I beg to assure you, Sir, that I used every effort to keep clear, but I could not have prevented the escape of the pirates without running some little risk by keeping close in to the reefs, which was entirely the cause of our getting ashore. We lost our chain cable anchor not being able to weigh it, but there appears to be only a little copper off her false keel.

He also tells us more about the pirate schooners:

> One of the pirate schooners mounts seven guns and the other five. They are both well fitted, sail remarkably well and only draw 5½ feet of water. They are well adapted for this part of the coast which is extremely dangerous for strangers and where I cannot attempt to get into with *Speedwell* as we draw nine feet of water.

His report ends with an explanation of what he was doing at Havana:

> I was obliged to put in here for water and in anticipation of meeting with either *Tyne* or *Sybille* for now that part of the coast is completely clear for a time and the Spanish squadron are still scouring the coast outside the Colorado where I cannot get to.

I have the honour to be, Sir, Your most obedient and humble servant
  William H. Geary

The faith of Geary that the Spanish squadrons of gun boats would keep the coasts of Cuba free of pirates is touching, but hardly likely to be shared by those Naval officers whose dispatches have already been seen and who had a good idea of the corrupt nature of Cuban officialdom. The report shows, nevertheless, that resolute action by even a little vessel commanded by a man of determination will always defeat piracy and keep the seas clear. The letter from Commander Cassis, to which Geary refers reads as follows:

> Sir, Permit me to tender you my acknowledgements for the co-operation of His Britannic Majesty's Schooner *Speedwell* under your command with the expedition dispatched from this ship the 30th Ultimo against several piratical vessels near the Bay of Honde and assure you of the pleasure with which it will be communicated to the United States Government by Very respectfully, Sir, Your obedient Servant
>   S. Cassis
>   Commanding US Ship *Peacock*

It is disappointing that there is no information about the fate of the pirate captain personally. Had he been captured by Geary and Cassis, one wonders what would have happened to him. Presumably, they would have had to leave him in the hands of the Cuban authorities as a Spanish subject. Then, he would probably have been able to pay a judge for his freedom in the way offered to Aaron. By escaping as he did, therefore, he simply saved the money. There were no grounds on which either the British or Americans could have dealt with him. They may have had difficulty in arguing that because he had committed offences against British and American ships and cargoes; he should be tried by either British or American courts.

American records also show us how the American Navy appreciated British help. In his book *Piracy in the West Indies*,[1] an American, Francis C. Bradley, refers to the cordial relationship between the two countries. He names a number of HM ships including HMS *Carnation*, commanded by Edward Walcot, and *Speedwell*.

Nevertheless, even between two friendly nations, there were differences in the way justice was administered. There was no doubt about the British attitude to piracy and, indeed, to slave trading. A British subject found guilty of either was on his way to the gallows.

Once America declared slave trading to be illegal, it was held to be piracy and punishable by hanging. Yet many Americans, particularly in the South, were opposed to the new law. Bradley refers to them in his book:

> ... in our country, these pirates had the sympathy, strange as it may seem, of many people to such an extent that very few were executed. Many, too, were captured a second time with their former comrades.

In spite of the differences, the story of USS *Peacock* shows us that the US Navy was intent on strong action against traditional pirates. Aaron tells us about the 'richly laden' *Peacock* of New York and how the pirate went in search of her. We can now see that this tempting prize was a decoy and that the US Navy

[1] *Piracy in the West Indies* by Francis B.C. Bradley,
The Essex Institute, Salem, Massachusetts, 1923.

was operating an under cover operation. Had she been found, Aaron would have been able to see how that Navy was working to eliminate piracy from those seas.

It is reasonable to assume that by the time Aaron came to trial at the Old Bailey, the full story of the action by *Speedwell* would have been known at the Admiralty. The prosecution may not have recognised its relevance to the case. On the other hand, had Aaron's counsel been informed of it, it might have come into the defence. There can be no doubt that one of the schooners was the one in which Aaron had been a prisoner. Suppose the evidence given by Septimus Hearn and others was the whole truth; that Aaron had not only become a willing member of the pirate crew, but had actually taken command. It would follow that he did not administer the sleeping draught and that the tale of the escape from the schooner in a canoe was pure fiction. He would then have been aboard the schooner in the Bay of Honde on 28th September.

There is no argument that he was arrested by the Spanish Officer who believed he had been cuckolded. But why would he scuttle a ship before he left the Bay of Honde? He did not know he was a wanted man, but even if he had, he would surely have stayed withthe schooner presenting himself as an innocent and wronged individual. He would have welcomed Geary and Cassis when they arrived on shore. He would have said how grateful he was to have been rescued from the awful life he had been forced to lead. The only conclusion to draw from this is that Aaron had already left by the time *Speedwell* and *Peacock* arrived on the scene and that his story is true. This evidence, presented in court, would have strengthened his defence.

Three
THE WEDDING & AFTER

The following is an extract from the marriage register of the Church of St Sepulchre, the parish church of Newgate prison:

> Aaron Smith of this parish, bachelor and Sophia Ann
> Knight of this parish, spinster, by Banns 23rd
> December 1823 by me, George Stoker LLB, Curate
> The marriage was solemnised between
> > Aaron Smith
> > Sophia Ann Knight
> In the presence of David Boast
> > Elizabeth Boast

After reading the *Faithful Narrative* written by Aaron and the story of how he reached the Old Bailey, this entry must have strong emotional overtones. Aaron had been tried for his life on Friday and was married on Tuesday

He had certainly been resident in the parish since the previous July, but in Newgate Gaol, and he would hardly have been free to go himself to see the Rev.

Stoker to arrange for the banns to be read. That must have been done by Sophia Knight. She is also shown as 'resident in the parish' and this tells us that she had come from her home in Sheerness to be near to Aaron and to give him all the comfort and help she could.

It so happens that while the custom of reading banns has its roots in pre-Christian practices, it had just been formalised in law in the Marriages Act of 1823. Under this then newly enacted measure, banns must be published in the parish(es) in which the parties reside or where they have resided for at least fifteen days before the first reading. They have to be read on three consecutive Sundays before the wedding can take place. This means that the first time of asking at St Sepulchre must have been not later than Sunday 7th December or, possibly, sooner. Sophia also had to have been living in the parish for at least fifteen days before that. We know, therefore, that she had come from Sheerness by not later than mid-November. By registering the banns, she showed faith in Aaron's innocence and a confidence that the wedding would be possible. This must have been a morale booster if nothing else.

The marriage register tells us something else in the signatures of David and Elizabeth Boast. He was the surgeon at Newgate ('the other Medical Gentleman') who also gave evidence at the trial in addition to Mr Holmes. One can assume that he showed Aaron sympathy. Otherwise, would he and his wife have been invited to the wedding and to act as witnesses?

At last, after the awful misery Aaron had suffered since his capture by the pirates, he had found support from friends on whom he could rely and who

wanted to help. It is reasonable to assume that Sophia
lodged with the Boasts throughout the months Aaron
was on remand.

The trial had been a 'show' piece. Admiral Rowley
could well have convened a Vice-Admiralty Court at
Jamaica and had Aaron tried there.

Perhaps it was the report from Commander Walcot
direct to the Admiralty that decided the venue. The
fact that the Attorney General himself led for the
prosecution suggests that the Admiralty wanted to
make a prominent example of Aaron in the hope that
it would deter others.

On the evidence available to the prosecution, the
case must have looked clear cut and unanswerable.

To modern lawyers, the hearing of seventeen witnesses in a trial not starting until eleven o'clock, is
quite remarkable. A case of this magnitude, today
would take several weeks.

Aaron's physical condition on arrival at Newgate
can be imagined. Being on remand, he would not have
been given any prison clothing. We know he had lost
all his possessions at the auction of property taken
from *Zephyr*. All he would have to wear would be the
clothes he had had in that infested gaol at Havana. If
it had been laundered and kept in repair, it might
have been bearable in the tropical climate of the West
Indies. But it was adequate neither for an English
winter nor aboard a frigate in the Atlantic where an
admiral had allowed him no comforts. The wounds on
his legs had been aggravated by being in irons. We
also know from what he tells us that he suffered
from attacks of a fever which sounds very much like
malaria.

When Sophia first saw him he must have been a

dreadful sight. Maybe she was the star witness at the trial. Maybe her production of that letter he had written before he left Jamaica, played a major role in securing the acquittal. Of equal importance must have been the part she played in giving him love and support when he needed it and in helping him to prepare his defence. What a difference there must have been between the wretched character who arrived at Newgate and the man described in *Morning Chronicle* as 'attired very gentlemanly in a suit of black' and by *The Times* the same day as 'very genteel'. No one suggests that Newgate Gaol was a convalescent home, but someone worked a miracle. It could be none other than Sophia. She would be aided, perhaps, by David Boast and Aaron's brother, William.

Aaron does not tell us why he went to Jamaica or why he stayed there for nearly two years. On the other hand, his brother William (not John as incorrectly reported by the *Morning Chronicle*), gave evidence to the effect that Aaron had a considerable sum of money and that he had intended to quit the sea.

To attempt to get at the truth behind this, it is necessary to rely on what might be called family folklore. Aaron's elder daughter, Sophia Jane Smith was married to the master mariner, Joseph Bennett of Liverpool. It was always believed in my family that her father, Aaron, had also been a seafarer, and that he had intended to leave the sea having amassed a 'fortune'. We were told that, alas, this 'fortune' had been lost in some kind of risky venture. When younger members of the family asked what this was, the answer was always to the effect that 'we do not talk about things of that sort.'

William gives us more than a clue to the true facts.

A Victorian family, jealous of its reputation for respectability, would never want to admit to having a relation who had been in the dock at the Old Bailey charged with piracy – even if he had got there through no fault of his own and was totally innocent. Even now, his great, great grandson, less inhibited by such things, has his leg pulled about having a 'pirate' for an ancestor. The distance between the generations is, of course, enough to make the taunts more light hearted. In any case, acquittal of a crime is not, today, by any means such a skeleton in the cupboard.

The evidence given by William Smith fits this family legend and gives us an idea of what Aaron's intentions were. His own account of trading in coffee at Jamaica; the purchase of turtles at Grand Cayman; his connection with Mr Watson, Ship's Chandler of London to whom the coffee aboard *Zephyr* was to be consigned; all point to ability as an entrepreneur and an intention to establish himself as an overseas trader dealing in imports and exports to and from the Caribbean area and, probably, working in the Baltic Exchange. Some of our great trading houses started in this way and around that time.

Whatever capital Aaron had accumulated for the establishment of his business would have gone in paying for his defence at the Old Bailey. He had not lost it exactly in the way the family pretended.

It is reasonable to assume that he and Sophia, united again and newly married, would have had a Happy Christmas together, but their prospects must have been grim. Aaron had to find a way of earning a living and supporting the wife who had been so loyal and helpful. Evidence of his worries is provided by a letter to the Admiralty and date stamped as having been received there on 27th December a week after the trial and, evidently, written over the Yuletide:

> My Lords,
>   Allow me to address your Lordships most respectfully and humbly beg to call Your Lordships consideration to the suffering of an *unfortunate* and *innocent* man. My Lords, a year has nearly elapsed since I should have been liberated in Havana had Your Lordships not have wished to try me by the Laws of England and during which time I have had to endure a very earthly misery as well as being entirely ruined through the enormous expense of searching for witnesses and as I can never suppose that Your Lordships had a wish to injure an innocent individual, I therefore beg leave with the greatest humiliation to throw myself upon Your Lordships clemency and humble hope that Your Lordships will pity my misfortune and make me some remuneration for my loss of time and my enormous expenses as I can assure Your Lordships that I am in the greatest distress.
>   Allow me to remain with great respect Your Lordships most obedient and humble servant.
>   Aaron Smith
>   PS. Please to address to me to the care of Mr Knight, Sheerness, Kent.

This letter is to be found at the Public Record Office under reference ADM1 5029. We know, therefore, that it was received, but there is no sign of a reply or even an acknowledgement.

Aaron's problems evidently continued. While some months later, he must have developed some plan for the future, he tried another approach to the Admiralty in a letter dated 8th July 1824:

> My Lords,
>   I have lately seen an account in the public papers of two American vessels being taken off the Island of Cuba by the pirates and the greatest part of the crews massacred. In order to put an end to those outrages I beg leave to make

you a tender of my services providing that you will make me a Master in the Navy or otherwise reward me suitably for my service and place me on board of a small vessel with 25 or 30 men and suitably armed and then I will forfeit my existence if a single vessel is captured between Cape San Antonio and Havana.

NB. I have no doubt that I should be able to take a great number of the people that have been aiding and assisting the late depredations. I am on the point of leaving England and should my services be excepted (sic) please to address to me the care of Mr Boast, Surgeon, New Kent Road, London. I remain with great respect Your Lordships most obedient and humble servant.

Aaron Smith

This offer was declined with thanks. It must have been written more in hope than expectation, particularly as he was already arranging to leave England and, presumably, to return to seafaring (or, as he says in the preface to his book – 'to be employed in the duties of his profession.' Perhaps the confidence of William Geary, that he had cleared the seas round Cape San Antonio for good, had been proved misplaced. Their Lordships, however, would have had no doubt that they had all the necessary resources at their disposal without commissioning a privateer. In any case, might it have occurred to them that, perhaps, after all, Aaron was guilty? If so, would it be safe to assume that a poacher could really become a gamekeeper?

The suggestion that he might 'take a great number of the people that have been aiding and assisting...' suggests that he had in mind another visit to Rio Medias. To say he wanted to see Seraphina again is, perhaps, unfair. It looks as if he still harboured his distrust of Royal Naval Officers' devotion to duty. Nevertheless, with the knowledge he must have had of the hazardous Colorado Shoal one wonders how he could believe he would be able to enter Rio Medias or any other similar pirate haven without the services of a local pilot.

It is interesting that Aaron was to be found lodging with his friends the Boasts. It may be he had come to London from Sheerness for the launch of his book published that year and he was about to return to the sea. He does not, however, come back into official records for another five years.

We are led to believe he had begun working in partnership with his brother William. This chap had been appointed as Master in the Royal Navy in January 1813 and had served until 16th November 1823 when he went on to half pay at six shillings per day. The naval record ADM11/3 tells us that while he was still able to serve, he suffered from a liver complaint and was often ill. His leaving the RN coincides with the latest possible date by which Sophia Knight arrived to be near Newgate. It is even probable that the two worked together in preparation of the defence, particularly in rounding up witnesses.

Sophia seems to have lived with her parents while Aaron was away at sea since two daughters, Sophia Jane and Lavinia were baptised together at Sheerness in May 1828 having been born, respectively, on 26th July 1826 and 7th May 1828. This suggests that Aaron was not absent at sea for long periods.

The couple must have had a hard time. In his book *Pirates of the Western Seas*, Captain Course, assumes the trial to be the end of Aaron's troubles. He comments that a seaman forced to become a pirate would receive fair consideration at the time in spite of the natural animosity and wish for vengeance that seaman had for pirates. This may be true, but what he does not say is that here was a man whose fortune was spent on his defence and whose plans for a future life with his wife and family were utterly destroyed. On the other hand, both Aaron and Sophia would have believed he was free at last. Little could they have known what further trouble lay ahead.

Four
BACK TO THE OLD BAILEY

If it is assumed that Aaron was intending to return to the sea when he wrote to the Admiralty in July 1824, it was certainly so by the beginning of 1829. That he was then working with his brother William is confirmed by what might be called a minor international diplomatic incident between Britain and the country then known as The Netherlands (later to be divided into Holland and Belgium). The arrival of a ship named *Louisa* at the Port of Antwerp started it all and brought Aaron a new problem.

According to Lloyd's Register for 1829, *Louisa* was a vessel of 400 tons built at Workington in 1810 and owned by Kains & Son of London. The master's name is given as 'Smith'. As there are neither initials nor forename, we cannot be sure whether Aaron or William was in command. All we can say for certain is that both were on board when, on 8th February 1829, she arrived at Cowes from Batavia. Lloyd's List also tells us that she then went on to Antwerp arriving there on 21st February having left Batavia on 10th

October 1828.

The cause of the excitement is explained in a letter to the British Foreign Office from The Netherlands and now held under reference F037/162 at the Public Record Office. It is dated from Brussels on 2nd March 1829 and reads:

> It appears that this Smith who arrived I believe from Cowes a short time ago at Antwerp in command of a British ship named *Louisa* which is still lying in that port was immediately upon his landing recognised by two persons as having in the year 1822 commanded a pirate vessel by which the ship in which they were members of the crew and which was named *La Prevoyante* was taken and being the person by whom they had on that occasion been most cruelly treated.
>
> Upon seeing that he was recognised, Smith it seems, contrived to escape and it is supposed that he is gone to England.
>
> From what I can collect ... the *Louisa* is thought at Antwerp to be a ship of rather a suspicious character, but I do not learn that any measures have been taken to prevent her departure.
>
> The brother of Smith who is now in command of the *Louisa* has I am told published a statement in the Antwerp newspapers declaring that his brother has only fled from thence in order that he might be tried, if tried he must be, by the Laws of his own country.

Maybe we cannot be sure who had been the master of *Louisa* – Aaron or William – but Aaron's flight makes good sense. He knew what he was doing. A trial in Antwerp, or anywhere else on the Continent, must have been loaded against him. The experience of his earlier trial would have shown him what it cost in money and effort to trace and assemble witnesses for the defence. Five years later, the task would be far greater and to have got them across the Channel might well have been beyond him. With a trial in

England, the prosecution would have more difficulty in that respect.

A fortnight later, there was a further despatch (ref F037/162) from the authorities in Antwerp to the Foreign Office in London. This was a lengthy document in French, but, translated, it included the following:

> ...this ship is commanded by William Smith, brother of the fugitive and will probably depart to-morrow for London. The ship is owned by a firm named Kain or Khain of London and has been here some time. I am told on good authority that the said Smith was seen on 8th March in Calais on his way to Dover.

The fact that *Louisa* arrived at London in May 1829 is confirmed by an unusual source – the record of the Receiver of Sixpences Account (ADM68/2109). Sixpence a month was deducted at that time from every seaman's wages for the benefit of Greenwich Hospital. The 'Register of Sixpences' survives at London and puts on record that the sixpences due from *Louisa* had been paid at Cowes in February.

From Lloyd's List, we also learn the reason for the suspicions regarding the character of the vessel. On arrival at Cowes it was reported that aboard *Louisa* four of the crew were dead and four were sick. There is, alas, no record to tell us how the deaths occurred or what was the nature of the illnesses. It is just one more example of the bad luck which dogged Aaron throughout those years. With Aaron gone, William must also have been short handed to say the least.

Aaron was arrested in April at 'lodgings in Stepney' and things began to move far more quickly than last time round. He came before the Thames magistrate on 24th April.

This hearing is of particular interest because the magistrate, a Mr Ballantyne, kept the proceedings secret in a foretaste of what we now know as reporting restrictions. He said he had reason to think that prejudice was caused to persons before their trial in cases of this kind. Details of the charges and the evidence by which they were supported by some means became public and often excited a vast outcry against the accused. He was resolved not to make himself a party to any such thing and had, therefore, determined to have the prisoner examined in a manner strictly private. He went on to demand from Aaron's legal adviser that if he allowed him to be present at the private examination, he would not give publicity to what had occurred. Mr Waller, Aaron's solicitor, gave this pledge. Aaron himself said nothing, but he and Mr Waller then retired with the Magistrate to a private room. After an examination of some hours, Aaron was remanded and committed for trial at the next Admiralty Session on charges of piracy.

Among the witnesses who had expected to be heard in open court was Captain Cooke of *Industry*. *The Times* reporter was clearly robbed of a lurid story by the magistrate's action and produced a tale which was totally irrelevant to the charge against Aaron. It tells how Captain Cooke, when commanding a ship named *Cambrian*, rescued the crew and passengers of *Kent*, an East Indiaman when she was on fire in the Bay of Biscay. The names of no other witnesses were given. Perhaps the report would serve to inflate Captain Cooke's ego, but little other purpose.

The authorities evidently tried to involve Septimus Hearn again. There is a letter from him in Admiralty records asking for a subsistence allowance for himself and his family since he was not 'available for employment'. This was refused on the grounds that the charge was brought not by any British authority, but by The King of The Netherlands. Perhaps this suggests that the trial proceeded without much official enthusiasm and mainly to avoid any diplomatic problems. Without the Dutch involvement, maybe there would never have been any second action at all. True or not, Aaron did not have to wait quite so long this time and he was allowed bail. He was back in the dock at the Old Bailey on 14th July 1829. There was a very full report of the trial in *The Times* the following day.

As before, there was preliminary consideration before a Grand Jury. The Lord Chief Justice of the Common Pleas, Sir Christopher Robinson presided and he began the proceedings with an address. This was reported in full in *The Times* the following day. The session was held, he said, for the purpose of bringing to trial a person charged with a very flagrant act of piracy on a Dutch ship in 1822 and who, since that period had been at large. It appeared that this person had been tried in 1823 for a piracy committed in the same part of the world. This, however, was a circumstance of which the special jury ought to discharge all recollection from their minds. The evidence now to be offered against the prisoner, so far as the Learned Judge was acquainted with it, was very strong.

... It was not competent to a Grand Jury to take defence into their consideration.

After hearing the evidence for the prosecution, the Grand Jury decided that there was, indeed, a prima facie case and brought in a true bill. Aaron, who had been on bail, then surrendered himself and the case proceeded.

The King's Advocate (or Counsel for the Prosecution – not the Attorney General, this time) immediately applied to the Court to postpone the trial on the grounds of the absence of a material witness who, having gone on a voyage to the East Indies, was not expected to arrive in this country for at least eight months. Aaron's Counsel opposed the application at considerable length and Sir Christopher Robinson ruled that, in the opinion of the Court, the trial ought to proceed at once.

The indictment was that 'on 14th July in the third year of the reign of his present Majesty (King George IV) Aaron Smith did piratically attack, set upon, board and break a ship called *Prevoyante* within about three leagues of the Island of Cuba on the high seas and within the jurisdiction of the Admiralty of England'.

The principal witness for the prosecution was Jacob Largethee, one of the Dutchmen who had spotted Aaron at Antwerp. He told the Court he had sailed from Antwerp for Havana with a cargo of butter, cheese, gin and linen. He described the capture of his ship in very much the manner already described by Aaron in his own account, but embellished his evidence with a description of the intervention of his 13-year-old son:

> ... two of the pirates laid hold of me and asked where the money was. They then put a rope round my neck and once again asked where the money was. I told them I had none. The pirates then fastened the end of the rope to an anchor. My son seized me by the breast and begged that he might be tied up with me. They dragged my poor boy from me and threw him down the hatches. They then threw me overboard holding me with one leg. My second mate grabbed me and dragged me back on board. When I came

166

up, I was quite senseless and was nearly strangled. I recovered a little after some time and the rope was gone from my neck. In stirring, I fell down in the forecastle...

Largethee is reported as speaking at length about the treatment he and his crew had received. He insisted several times that Aaron was in total and voluntary command of all that happened. He even told the court that it was Aaron who had allowed him to leave so long as he never put in at Havana saying that if ever he went there, 'he would kill me'.

We can read this evidence in the knowledge of Aaron's own description of Largethe's panic when he was in the hands of the pirate.

Counsel for the defence, a Mr Broderick, then cross examined. In answer to the first question, he said:

There were 40 men on board the pirate schooner and Smith appeared to be the best seaman among them. When my boy was wounded on board, Smith was in the schooner.

Mr Broderick:

Now answer me this question. Did not Mr Smith, a few days after the capture of your vessel, tell you that he was the mate of an English vessel and tell you he was compelled to act towards you as he was doing?

Largethee:

Yes, about eight days after I was captured, Smith called me aside and said that he was the chief mate of an English vessel: that he was compelled by force to take part with the pirates. He also informed me that it was owing to him my ship was taken; for that his spy glass at once showed that my vessel was a trader. When I was going away, Smith merely repeated to me in English what the pirates had told

me in Spanish – namely that if any of the pirate cruisers
found me going to Havana, they would certainly kill me.
Smith always used his own name.

This appeared to have made Largethee shift his
position a little and, in reply to a further question
prompted by Aaron, he agreed that:

Smith was in command of the boat which saved the man
who was thrown overboard.

Once again, Aaron was allowed to address the jury. *The
Times* reports that he did this with 'much feeling and
ability'. He entered, the paper tells us, into a history
of his life from the time he left England until he was
captured by the pirate schooner, on board which he
was when *Prevoyante* was taken. He was himself driven on board the pirate at the point of a sword and was
compelled to act in whatever way the pirates ordered
him. When taken by the pirates he was under an
engagement to be married to a young lady; that lady
was examined at his former trial and proved the fact.
She had, however, now become his wife and he must
therefore lose the benefit of her testimony on this
occasion. There were other witnesses examined at the
former trial whose evidence he would now produce.

Captain Cowper, who was a passenger aboard
Zephyr was the first witness for the defence and he
gave a full description of how Captain Lumsden had
been forced to let Aaron be taken prisoner. William
Foster, who was a seaman aboard *Zephyr* also told how
the pirates had threatened to cut off Aaron's head if he
did not go with them quietly.

Another witness whose name is not given began
giving evidence to the same effect when there was a

development which cannot have happened often in any British Court of Law. The jury interrupted the proceedings. They declared that, in their opinion, Smith was not a free agent during any part of the transactions with *Prevoyante*. The Court was of the same opinion and a verdict of not guilty was returned.

The Times concludes its report with the words:

> There were several other witnesses in attendance on behalf of Mr Smith, but the interference of the jury prevented their being examined.

At last, Aaron was a free man.

It may appear strange that there is no appearance at either trial by Lumsden, Captain of *Zephyr*. Surely Aaron would have tried to get him to give evidence of his capture from the vessel. The final words of Aaron's own book do not name Lumsden, but they give us a clue that he had:

> ...not the common feeling of humanity ... to come forward himself in my behalf; and God forbid that such should ever fall to the lot of any man.

Five
EPILOGUE

After the 1829 trial, Aaron disappeared from public record for twenty-one years. He may have been a free man, but, even now, he was not to be completely finished with the law courts. He may well have regarded Lumsden as lacking any degree of friendship, but he had an implacable enemy in the person of Captain Cooke of *Industry*.

His partnership with brother William aboard *Louisa* probably began after the first trial and it seems that she was engaged in trade with the Far East as is suggested by her arrival at Cowes from Java. The vessel, however, was sold by Kains & Son in 1830. Since her name is not mentioned in any Lloyd's List, it is reasonable to assume she passed into foreign ownership.

Had Aaron continued seafaring until 1835, we would expect to find reference to him in the Register of Seamen which came into being that year. Since there is no such record, it is probable that he and William parted company soon after the second trial.

There are reports of his living in London and in business as an underwriter and as a bill discounter. He came to public notice again on 31st January 1850 when he attended a meeting in the London Tavern called to petition Parliament to abolish what was called 'head money' for Borneo pirates. This was cash paid by the Government in lieu of prize money for pirates officially sworn to have been killed. There were suggestions that it was being improperly paid; that humble fishermen and others picked up on shore were killed so that people in high places – including a rajah – were lining their pockets.

Aaron, described now as a burly seafaring man, stood up at the meeting to contradict this saying that pirates were very real; that he himself had once been attacked and his ship nearly taken. The meeting, and Aaron's contribution to it, were referred to during a debate on the Navy Estimates in the House of Commons on 23rd May 1850. Richard Cobden MP for West Riding (Hansard Col 303 of that date) claimed to know about 'Captain Aaron Smith' who, he said, was an 'atrocious pirate'. He had heard from a Captain Cooke who could prove it. When he heard about this, Aaron asked for a meeting with Cobden, but was refused. As a result there began an angry correspondence in *The Times* and Captain Cooke eventually wrote a letter in which he said Aaron was 'certainly a pirate and should be punished as such'. Aaron then issued a writ for libel. The subsequent trial was almost a re-run of the two earlier trials except that most of the defence witnesses were dead or lost from contact. It seems, however, that Aaron had lost none of his powers of persuasion and he won the case even though damages were small.

William Smith was still on half pay from the Royal Navy and, therefore, the Admiralty knew where to find him. Their record (PMG 15/25.5O) tells us that in 1846 he was living in Cork; in 1856 in Dublin; that he moved to Falmouth in 1858 where he died on 21st October 1862. There was no vast fortune involved since the same record shows his estate as 'being less than £100'.

The story of Aaron Smith came to light as a result of research into the career of Joseph Bennett, Master Mariner of Liverpool. By the age of 23, Aaron's elder daughter, Sophia Jane was in Liverpool as his wife and as mother of what was to become a family of five children.

To Sophia Jane's grandchildren, we know, Aaron Smith was a skeleton to be kept in the cupboard and not to be talked about. To have had a relative who had been in the dock twice at Old Bailey court could do nothing for one's respectibility even if he was acquitted and later won an action in the civil court. There was far less inhibition about the career of Joseph Bennett. It was accepted in the family that he had been captain of a slave ship carrying wretched human cargoes across the Atlantic. Maybe the story was told without great pride, but there was no sense of shame. One has to remember that the Port of Liverpool had virtually been founded on slave trading. At one time, and certainly within the living memory of the Bennett family, the trade had had considerable support. It was even supposed that it was supported by some passages in the Bible and many clergymen of the early 19th century gave it their blessing. In 1808, however, twelve years before Joseph Bennett was born, slave trading, as opposed to slavery itself, became illegal. Then, and particularly after the end of the Napoleonic wars, the

Royal Navy was vigilant against transgressors.

For several years, Joseph Bennett was in command of the brigantine *Daybreak* which had been built at Prince Edward Island in the Maritime Provinces of Canada. In her, he plied regularly between Liverpool and the West Coast of Africa (the Slave Coast). The ship's logs are held in the Public Archives at Charlottetown PEI and they give details of all her voyages. He must have seen something of illegal trading by others – particularly the Spanish and Portuguese – but for an English merchant captain to risk capture by a Royal Naval patrol would have been very foolhardy. Arrest would have been to secure a one way passage to Execution Dock at Wapping.

The stories told by his grandchildren (my mother and her sisters) led me into research which has failed to reveal any hard evidence that Joseph Bennett had been directly, at least, involved in slave trading. Nevertheless, the baptism record of Sophia Jane led me to her father and the full story which is told here.

NOTE. Those convicted by an Admiralty Court of piracy, mutiny on the high seas or slave trading would be taken to the gallows at Execution Dock at Wapping. Anyone who has taken a Thames River launch from Westminster or the Embankment to Greenwich will have had the site pointed out by the boatman.

The gallows were set at low water mark so that after the hanging, the body would be slowly submerged by the incoming tide. It would not be moved until three tides had come and gone. Execution Dock was the scene of capital punishment for more than four centuries until the last execution in 1830 – just after Aaron's second trial.

GENEALOGY

Aaron Smith was born at Huggate, North Yorkshire in 1796. His parents were John Smith and Jane-née Cross. Father lived to the ripe old age of 93 and died in 1855. Jane died in 1840 at the age of 69.

In the register of baptisms held at The Borthwick Institute of Historical Research at York, Aaron's father is described as a labourer. The Cross family, however, were yeoman farmers and there are a number of records showing awards of rights in land and pasture over generations. At one time, they were regarded as the leading family in the district.

John and Jane had three children. William, was born in 1791, Ann in 1793 and Aaron. There is nothing in the family history to show any attachment to the sea, but, as we know, both the boys were to be sailors.

BIBLIOGRAPHY

There are countless books about pirates, buccaneers, privateers, corsairs and filibusters to be found in libraries all over the world. In addition there are papers to be found in The Public Record Office, National Maritime Museum and similar places. More details are to be found in ships' log books, trial documents and newspapers. It is sometimes difficult to differentiate between fact, fiction and 'faction' since piracy is surrounded by myth and folklore.

So far as this book is concerned, there is no reason to doubt its veracity and the following works have been helpful.

Allen, Gardner W. *Our Navy and the West Indian Pirates*. Essex Institute, Salem Massachusetts. 1929

Bradlee, Frances B.C. *Piracy in the West Indies & Its Suppression*. Essex Institute, Salem, Mass.1923.

Clowes, William Laird, *The Royal Navy, A History* Vol VI. Simpson. Low, Marston & Co., London, 1901.

Cordingley, David. *Life Among the Pirates*. Little,

Brown & Co. London. 1995

Course, Captain A.G. *Pirates of the Western Seas*
Frederick Muller, London, 1969
(It was this book which began my researches.There is
a chapter entitled Jean Lafitte and Aaron Smith and
this was the first hint I had that he had anything to do
with pirates).

Thrower, Rayner *The Pirate Picture* Bowman &
Millfield, New Jersey, 1980.

Ward, W.E.F. *The Royal Navy & The Slavers*
George Allen & Unwin Ltd, London. 1969

APPENDIX

Extracts from Lloyd's Lists and Lloyd's Registers regarding the three principal British merchant vessel victims mentioned in Aaron Smith's account.

Zephyr. Brig 170 tons. Built Whitehaven by Wm Bowes. Launched, 1st October 1818. Owner, Hammond.
She was ultimately lost near Lisbon in 1842. Her departure date from England does not seem to be recorded, but other vessels arriving at Jamaica, also from Cork, about the same date sailed from English ports in late December 1821. She arrived Jamaica from Cork 16th February 1822.
Lloyd's List dated 27th August 1822:-
Zephyr (Lumsden) arrived The Downs (off Kent) yesterday (Monday 26th August) from Jamaica and Havana, was boarded 7th ultimo off Cape San Antonio by a schooner with two guns and with 35 men which plundered and threw overboard a considerable part of the cargo, materials etc.
Captain Lumsden was obliged to give the pirates

doubloons and silver to the value of £1,500 to prevent them from burning the ship. Two passengers were robbed and the mate was retained on board.

Vittoria.

A snow (similar to a brig rig) 242 tons. Built Whitehaven by Wm Bowes. Launched 26th August 1813: Owner Cohen & Co.

Lloyd's List 8 November 1822 No 5749:-

Date line Charleston, America. 2nd October 1822. The brig *Vittoria* of and for London from Jamaica, a captured vessel has laid inside the Colorados (W.Cuba) as a storeship for upwards of six weeks. The coffee of this and other vessels finds its way to the port of Havana: it is taken out of the casks and introduced into the city in bags by launches in open air and sold.

Vittoria is listed by Lloyds up to 1825 but is dropped from the 1826 Register.

Industry

Lloyd's List 11th October 1822 – 5741 St Thomas: arrived *Industry* (Cook) from Jamaica after brig taken and plundered by a piratical schooner. No dates given

CHRONOLOGY

22 Nov. 1790 John Smith (labourer) married Jane
Cross at Huggate Yorks.

20 Mar. 1796 Aaron Smith baptised at Huggate,
Yorks.Son of John and Jane Smith.

13 Jan. 1813 William Smith applied to Admiralty
for appointment as Master.

19 Jul. 1821 *Harrington* sailed from Gravesend with
Aaron Smith as Mate.

19 Sep. 1821 *Harrington* arrived at Bermuda.

16 Feb. 1822 *Zephyr* arrived Jamaica from Cork.

Jun. 1822 (no day given) Aaron Smith wrote to
Sophia Knight to say he was coming
home in *Zephyr* in order to marry her.

29 Jun. 1822 *Zephyr* sailed from Jamaica with
Aaron Smith as mate.

7 Jul. 1822 *Zephyr* boarded by pirates and Smith
taken prisoner.

14 Jul. 1822 *Preyovant* (Dutch) attacked by pirates.

7 Aug. 1822 *Industry* and *Vittoria* boarded.

10 Aug. 1822 HMS *Carnation* met Industry and took

	on board the crew of *Vittoria*
29 Sep.1822	HMS *Speedwell* & USS *Peacock* attacked pirates in Bay of Honde.
3 Oct. 1822	Admiral Rowley wrote to Captain General of *Cuba* demanding action against pirates and Smith in particular.
16 Mar 1823	Captain Lillicrap (HMS *Hyperion*) also asked for Smith's arrest.
3 May 1823	HMS *Sybille* took Smith aboard as prisoner.
28 Jun. 1823	Smith discharged from *Sybille* to *Genoa*
4 Jul. 1823	Smith discharged to Thames Police.
16 Nov. 1823	William Smith left the RN.
19 Dec. 1823	Trial at Old Bailey.
23 Dec. 1823	Aaron Smith and Sophia Knight Married at St Sepulchre, 'a parish in London adjoining the Middlesex Parish of Clerkenwell'.
2 Mar. 1829	Report to Foreign Office re Smith's arrival at Antwerp.
16 Mar. 1829	Letter in French re William Smith being in command of *Lousia*
24 Apr. 1829	*Times* report of second committal proceedings.
14 Jul. 1829	Second trial on charge brought by King of the Netherlands.

BRIG

A two-masted vessel fully square rigged on both masts with a fore-and-aft sail on the lower part of the mainmast.

SCHOONER

A two-masted vessel fore-and-aft rigged on both masts.